The
MOSAIC BOOK

The MOSAIC BOOK
Ideas, Projects and Techniques

PEGGY VANCE and CELIA GOODRICK-CLARKE

Special photography by
CLAY PERRY

Trafalgar Square Publishing
NORTH POMFRET, VERMONT

With thanks to my husband,
Dharminder Singh Kang.
Peggy Vance

First published in the United States of America in 1995 by
Trafalgar Square Publishing, North Pomfret, Vermont 05053

First published 1994 by
Conran Octopus Limited, 37 Shelton Street, London WC2H 9HN

Project Editors Jo Mead and Louise Simpson
Copy Editor Jo Mead
Art Editor Alison Fenton
Design Ian Muggeridge
Special Photography Clay Perry
Colour Illustrations Alison Barrett
Design Assistant Alison Barclay
Motif Illustrations King & King
Picture Researcher Abigail Ahern
Editorial Assistant Tessa Clayton
Production Controller Mano Mylvaganam
Research & Layout for Motifs Louise Hillier

Library of Congress Catalog Card Number: 94-60798

ISBN 1-57076-015-2

Printed and bound in Singapore by Tien Wah Press

CONTENTS

FOREWORD

Working as a journalist in the interior design field, I have had the good
fortune during the last twelve years to visit hundreds of fascinating
homes all over the world. Many of them, I came to realize, were distinguished by the use of mosaic decoration, either as decorative
embellishment or as a work of art proudly displayed. Once conscious
of the medium, you realize it's a familiar sight everywhere: on the bot-
tom of swimming pools, on the sides of the Underground station, glit-
tering behind bars at restaurants, or discreetly colouring the floors of
sober banks. I have even seen Cornish villages adorned with pebbles,
shells and bright chippings of tile and glass.

And yet mosaic is not a mere designer accessory that relates purely
to twentieth-century style. Mosaic is the oldest, most durable and

most functional art form, with
colours that never fade, and materials that withstand sun, rain,
frost or even centuries of burial.
Carlo Bertelli says in his famous
book *Mosaics*, 'mosaic art flows
through history like a great river
through a porous desert, disap-
pearing and reappearing again'.
Colours in early mosaics tended
to be of natural stone: soft greens,
blue, ochre, white, terracotta and
black, but gradually highlights of
glass were added. A dazzling kaleidoscope of colour was introduced
with glass smalti by the Byzantine masters, who found that by angling
smalti in the mortar they could create brilliant plays of light on the
surface patterns. The ancients also believed that glancing lights and
shards of mirror contained a 'flash of spirit'. Which is why outdoor
mosaics look so lovely in the rain, gleaming amongst the wet foliage.

In principle, mosaic is simple to create – it can be tackled by anyone who can tile a wall or glue down a collage. In practice, it needs to

be carefully conceived, designed, planned and executed for a really professional finish. For any beginner, there is one important point to remember: the simple design is the best design. A complete novice might start with something that is regular and flat, such as a mirror surround (*see* pp.42–3), or that does not take long to complete, such as small-scale jewellery (*see* pp.52–5).

On a final note, I think it is important to stress that the projects we have chosen are really intended to be inspirational ideas to provoke a little lateral thinking and increase your understanding and appreciation of this exciting art form. Enjoy!

Celia Goodrick-Clarke

THE GLORIOUS LEGACY

At heart we are perhaps all mosaicists, for who can resist the temptation to colour in noughts, fit the last piece of a jigsaw or make patterns with loose buttons or sweets.

The ancient art of mosaic derives from just such a basic desire for order and ornamentation. Five thousand years ago the Sumerians created mural patterns by driving coloured clay cones into walls, and by the third century B.C. the Greeks were constructing representational mosaics out of variously coloured uncut pebbles. Since these early times man has used 'bits' of stone, ceramic, glass, shell, plastic and many other more unusual materials to create mosaics for public and private buildings, spaces and purposes. The variety of possible applications is tremendous, including interior and exterior schemes, furniture, jewellery and an enormous range of decorative objects.

The permanence of the materials used has meant that much mosaic has survived in good condition, including many exceptional Roman works. Inspired by Hellenistic examples, the Romans exploited the functional and decorative qualities of the medium to the full, using it both for hardwearing pavimental and intricate mural decoration. Mosaics have been found across the entire area of the Roman Empire exhibiting an enormous range of genres and styles – from conventionalized compositions depicting the gods to closely observed scenes of everyday life, simple monochrome 'silhouette' images, detailed studies of animals and an inexhaustible repertoire of abstract border and infill designs.

During the reign of Emperor Justinian (A.D. 518–27) Roman, Barbarian and Eastern influences contributed to the fruition of the

The panel depicting the Triumph of Neptune (below left), which dates from the first half of the third century A.D., demonstrates the sophistication of late Roman mosaic in the fineness of its tesserae, its close description of anatomical and other detail, and the broad, sinuous sweep of its composition.

The popularity of pavimental mosaics across the Roman Empire can be attributed both to technical advances that allowed for swifter production and to the fact that the Romans quarried enormous quantities of local marble wherever they went. The Moroccan pavement (below) accords with the convention for emblemata – more intricately worked panels – to be inserted

within a dense framework of abstract border designs.

The presbytery of San Vitale in Ravenna contains two outstanding panels depicting Emperor Justinian and Empress Theodora. In the former (opposite), glass smalti, precious and semi-precious stones are used to convey the splendour of the robed and crowned Emperor and his retinue.

Byzantine style. Christian pictorial conventions were becoming well-established, with a hierarchy of images evolving in response to the encouragements of patronage. Mosaic fast became a primary medium for the decoration of Christian churches, a natural extension of the Byzantine practice of cladding walls with a decorative marble skin.

The mosaics of the church of San Vitale in Ravenna, the last Imperial capital of Italy, consummately illustrate the accomplishments of the period: the unfettered use of vibrant colour (including the introduction of gold smalti); the combining of different materials; and the creation of an undulating surface that exploits reflection.

FERDINANDO III ET M.CAROLINAE REGINAE
PIISSIMIS CLEMENTISSIMIS
INTER AMORES ET VOTA SICILIAE
QUA PIETATE POTEST MAXIMA ET ANIMO
VICTO PERMAGNIS BENEFICIIS OMNIA

The fashion for mosaic to imitate painting reached a peak in the eighteenth century when large mosaic panels were executed that employed similar compositions and an enormous 'palette' of painterly hues (left).

Art Nouveau, and particularly its Catalan offshoot, modernisme, resulted in many civic buildings being adorned with an exuberant agglomeration of abstract and stylized pattern (below).

Mosaic was integral to Antonio Gaudí's distinctive architecture, used as a dynamic and expressive means of colouring form (opposite).

The Byzantine style of fifth- and sixth-century Ravenna was to be sustained and developed in Venice and to reach its ultimate expression in Constantinople, the centre of Orthodox Christianity, between the thirteenth and fifteenth centuries.

Initially, the Renaissance saw a decline in the practice of mosaic, but by the mid-fifteenth century large quantities of smalti were being produced in Murano, and new works were created influenced by contemporary developments in painting.

A fascinating dialogue ensued between painting and mosaic, each medium imitating the other and striving to create illusionistic effects. Panels were worked with tesserae so fine as to have a seemingly smooth texture and church interiors were frequently painted in imitation of gold mosaic.

But it was in the late sixteenth century that Renaissance mosaic reached its apogee in the enormous works for St Peter's Basilica in Rome, their compositions suffused with the painterly qualities that made Ghirlandaio (as reported by Vasari) remark that mosaic was *'La vera pittura per l'eternità'* (the true way of painting for eternity).

By the eighteenth century Rome was firmly established as a great centre for mosaic, a studio having been set up within the Vatican, the primary aim of which was to produce further monumental works for St Peter's. At the same time as these massive panels were being executed, however, there also existed in Rome a vogue for miniature mosaic using tesserae barely visible to the naked eye.

The eclectic historicism of the nineteenth century fuelled a revival of arts and crafts of all kinds, including mosaic, which became increasingly widely practised, with dedicated schools springing up to serve large public commissions (including St Paul's Cathedral in London and the Paris Opera). The famous workshop of Antonio Salviati in Murano was a particular success, producing fine reproductions of historic mosaics for worldwide export.

At the turn of the century, however, the burgeoning Art Nouveau movement began to loosen the ties that had bound mosaic to an imitative, representational language, allowing the introduction of pure pattern, abstracted and stylized forms. Relatively ordinary buildings in major cities, most notably Paris, Barcelona and Prague, developed a

'rash' of mosaic decoration, and Barcelona in particular was distinguished by the exuberant and idiosyncratic creations of the architect Antonio Gaudí. His influence was to forge a path towards complete freedom of expression in mosaic, encouraging such artists as Klimt, Chagall and Kokoschka to design for this most enduring of media.

TOOLS AND MATERIALS

Tesserae

These are the basic building blocks that form the mosaic. At the start of any mosaic project it is advisable to have planned and prepared sufficient tesserae to complete it. Listed below are the most common types, but to these may be added a host of other objects and materials, including semi-precious stones, shells, buttons, *faux* gems and pearls.

Smalti These rectangular chunks of opaque glass – generally 10 x 15 x 7 mm (⅜ x ½ x ¼ in) are hand-made in Italy, available in an enormous range of colours, and offer an irregular, highly light-reflective surface. Sold by the half kilo, they are of a standard price regardless of their colour, although gold and silver (plain or 'ripple') are more expensive, having finely beaten precious metal sandwiched between a thick layer of coloured glass and a thinner veneer of plain glass. These may be used with either side uppermost, depending upon the effect desired; their standard size is 20 x 20 x 4 mm (¾ x ¾ x 3/16 in).

Vitreous glass These lozenges of opaque glass – 20 x 20 x 4 mm (¾ x ¾ x 3/16 in) – are smooth on the front and slightly corrugated on the back to provide key. Their range of colours is not quite as wide as that of smalti, but they are strong, less expensive (though the price of different colours varies), highly weather resistant and very easy to cut with nippers (*see* p.13). These tesserae may be bought loose in a mixed bag, in single colours, or stuck face down on paper, making them ideal for the indirect method (*see* pp.18–19).

Marble Although somewhat difficult to cut (*see* p.13), marble offers a fantastic natural range of colours and patterns. It may either be polished or left matt, in which case it should be sealed.

Stones and pebbles Hard stones are preferable, e.g. flints, quartz, granite and limestone. Stones and pebbles should be deeply embedded in a cement base.

Ceramic tesserae These range from plain white household tiles, which may be painted and fired, to small earthenware tiles and broken crockery. Whilst the variety is endless, and the material generally easy to cut, ceramic can be vulnerable to frost.

Tesserae-cutting tools, tesserae-fixing glues and adhesives, and health and safety equipment (above). Clockwise from top: scalpel; Stanley knife; palette knife; glass cutter; general-purpose engineer's pliers; flat-edged pliers; spring-loaded nippers; hammer; dust mask; goggles; scissors; brown paper; cement tile adhesive; gum arabic; PVA adhesive; rubber spatula.

The most traditional and most effective of tools for cutting smalti, marble and stone, the hammer and hardie (the latter sometimes called a bolster blade) may only be purchased from specialist suppliers (see p.126). In order to provide a firm and secure cutting edge, the hardie is generally embedded in the sawn-off end of a log and for added durability both the distinctive, curved hammer and the hardie may be tipped with tungsten carbide. To cut a tessera, hold the mosaic material between the thumb and finger of the left hand (or right hand for left-handers), its longest edge across the blade. Hold the hammer in the right hand (or left for left-handers), positioned so as lightly to strike the mosaic material directly above the hardie blade's edge. Practice is required to master accurate cutting.

Tesserae-cutting tools

In addition to the primary tools below, most mosaicists will find it useful to have pliers, a glass cutter and a hammer.

Nippers (mosaic cutters or tile nippers). These are ideal for fashioning vitreous glass and ceramic into fairly precise shapes (*see* p.17). The spring-loaded variety is less arduous for long-term use.

Hammer and hardie A traditional tool, comprising an anvil and a hammer, (*see* caption above) used primarily for cutting marble and smalti. Ideally, both parts should be tungsten-tipped for strength, and the hammer should be in proportion with the size of the hardie.

Supports and bases

Most surfaces are receptive to mosaic if prepared correctly. Metal should be scored or coated to give it key and wood should be sealed. Medium density fibreboard (MDF) or plyboard of approximately 12.5 mm (½ in) thickness is popular as a support because it is strong, durable and warp-resistant.

Glues and adhesives

The glues and adhesives used should be suitable both for the tesserae and the base. PVA (polyvinyl acetate) adhesive is excellent for sticking glass and ceramics to wood; interior cement-based tile adhesive for ceramics to wood and synthetics; water-resistant cement-based tile adhesive for ceramics to metal or concrete for exterior siting; silicone sealant for ceramics to glass; epoxy resin for glass to metal; marble mastic for marble to most surfaces; and gum arabic and wallpaper paste for the temporary bonding of tesserae to paper (*see* pp.18–19).

Cement and grout

Cement may be used as a medium for affixing tesserae to a base or may constitute the base itself (*see* pp.18–19). It is made of one of various types of crushed stone which, when combined with water and sand, forms a substantial, cheap and strong support. It may be applied to walls (*see* pp.98–9) or set as slabs (*see* pp.90–3), and is suitable for siting outdoors so long as it is allowed to dry out slowly in frost-free conditions (cement additives, such as waterproofer and frost protective, can increase its resilience).

Grout is used to fill the interstices between the tesserae (*see* p.17). Many mosaicists consider ungrouted work to be more expressive, but grouting strengthens the bond to the base and creates a practical, smooth surface. Different grouts are appropriate for different tasks, but all may be coloured with water-based tempera or acrylic paint added to the dry mix. Grout should be cleaned from the surface of the tesserae before it dries with a sponge or

stiff brush or, if stubborn, a dilute solution of hydrochloric acid after twenty-four hours.

Safety note

Goggles should be worn when cutting tesserae and a mask when cutting tesserae, sawing fibreboard or using solvents. Rubber gloves are advised for all procedures involving cement, grout and acid.

Mosaic tesserae (opposite). In the centre, smalti beneath shards of ceramic tile. Clockwise from top: mirror glass; faux gems; pebbles; silver and gold smalti; vitreous glass tesserae; glitter.

Cementing and grouting tools and materials (above). Clockwise from top: sponge; notched float; paintbrushes; chisel; nailbrush; rubber gloves; cement; grout colourant; sand; mixed cement; trowel; squeegee; lint-free cloth.

THE DIRECT METHOD: CHESSBOARD

This is the most basic and adaptable technique for the laying of mosaic. Tesserae are stuck face-up into a prepared ground, and whether using smalti, vitreous glass, marble or ceramic, on bases as varied as wood, metal, stone or net, the process is essentially the same. Great virtue can be made of slight irregularities in the surface created, particularly when smalti or other light-reflective tesserae are used or when less orthodox pieces – for instance the handles of smashed crockery – are a feature, and many direct works are therefore left ungrouted. This method may be employed equally well on a small scale, as demonstrated here by Martin Cheek's stylish chessboard, or

1

for more sizable commissions for public spaces. The most appropriate uses of the direct method are when the mosaicist needs to be able to monitor the work from the front, or when the subject to be covered is three-dimensional, so that the mosaic 'skin' has to wrap around it.

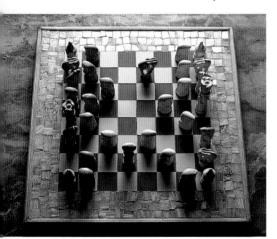

2

Materials
64 ceramic (Portuguese Cinca) tiles
Veined vitreous glass tesserae
Medium density fibreboard (MDF) or plyboard, approximately 26cm² (10¼in²)
PVA adhesive
'Hockey stick' framing wood
Gimp pins (small tacks)
Wood filler (plastic wood)
Wood stain (optional)
Dry grout
Water-based paint
Liquid floor cleaner

Tools
Nippers
Jigsaw
Saw or scalpel
Sand paper
Pencil
Ruler
Mixing board
Jug
Trowel
Squeegee
Lint-free cloth
Rubber gloves
Toothpick

1 Cut two glass tesserae into quarters (see step 3) using the nippers and lay out one full row of eight ceramic tiles with three of the quartered glass tesserae on either side. Leave small gaps in between the pieces for grouting.

Measure the row of tiles and tesserae and cut the medium density fibreboard or plyboard into a square of the same dimension with a jigsaw. Prime the board on both sides with a bonding agent made of 50% PVA and 50% water. Leave for an hour.

Key the board with a saw or scalpel. Cut four lengths of 'hockey stick' framing wood, mitre the ends, glue them to the board and tack them into place with two gimp pins (small tacks) on

3

4

5

6

5 Wearing rubber gloves, place a small quantity of dry grout on to a board and make a well in its centre. Should you wish to colour the grout use a small quantity of a water-based (acrylic or tempera) paint (*see* pp.14–15). Gradually pour in cold water, blending it into the grout with a trowel until the mixture has a malleable consistency like soft butter.

6 Trowel a large dollop of grout on to the surface of the chessboard and spread it across with a squeegee. Ensure that there is a good, even covering and that all the crevices have been filled, then immediately wipe the surface of the board with a slightly damp lint-free cloth to remove the excess. Wipe in this way until the surface is virtually clean. Ensure too that the frame is clear of any smudges of grout. Pick off any grout remaining on the surface of the tesserae with a matchstick or toothpick. Leave to dry for 24 hours and polish with a liquid floor cleaner.

each side. Fill any gaps with wood filler, sand the corners to remove roughness and finally stain the frame if you wish.

2 Draw a cross and diagonals on the board to act as a positioning guide. Now 'butter' the backs of the ceramic tiles with PVA adhesive and stick them down to align with the diagonals (leaving small gaps for grouting). Start in the centre and let the pattern 'grow' outwards.

3 Once the chessboard area is complete, cut the rest of the vitreous glass into quarters with the nippers. These tools require a little practice to master – hold the nippers squarely between the thumb and forefinger of one hand and place the 'teeth' at a right angle to the middle edge of the tessera. Nip them together – the tessera should snap cleanly in two rectangles. (If you want to produce two triangles, use the nippers diagonally in the corner of the square.)

4 Start to stick down the outer ring of vitreous glass tesserae ridge-side down with the veining of each running in a different direction to give an interesting texture. When this is complete, stick down the next two rings together to fill the remaining space evenly. Leave to dry for at least one hour.

THE INDIRECT METHOD: PAVING SLAB

This method primarily developed in order that large-scale work could be undertaken off-site for reasons of accessibility and convenience. As with the direct method (*see* pp.16–17), the materials employed may vary but the basic principle remains the same, as demonstrated here by Martin Cheek's paving slab: the mosaicist sticks the tesserae face down and in reverse on to a temporary support using an impermanent bonding agent (water-based glue). A permanent base (usually cement) is then prepared into which the tesserae are set and the temporary support is finally peeled away to reveal the front of the mosaic for the first time. The resultant mosaic surface is likely to be

1

far flatter than that produced using the direct method. This is a great advantage when creating smooth finishes and is ideal for floors. Mosaics made using the indirect method are invariably grouted in order to enhance their smoothness and durability and to make them easy to clean.

2

Materials	Tools		
Brown paper	*Pencil and pens*		*Rubber gloves*
Brown paper tape	*Ruler*		*Jug*
Medium density	*Nippers*		*Snips*
fibreboard (MDF)	*Saw*		*Trowel*
or plyboard 25.5cm²	*Wooden battens,*		*Plastic sheeting*
(10in²)	*5 x 2.5cm (2 x 1in)*		*Squeegee*
Vitreous glass tesserae	*in section*		*Lint-free cloth*
in contrasting tones	*Drill*		*Household brush or*
Gum arabic or	*Screws, 3.25cm (1¼in)*		*non-metal kitchen*
wallpaper paste	*long*		*scourer*
Petroleum jelly	*Artist's paintbrush*		
Fine sand			
Chicken wire			
Cement			
Dry grout			

1 Soak a 23cm (9in) square of brown paper in water and stretch it over the medium density fibreboard or plyboard, securing it tautly with brown paper tape. Once the paper has dried, draw on it in pencil the 20.5cm² (8in²) outer square of the paving slab. Then draw in the basic design of the slab, marking in a separate colour to distinguish the different areas of the pattern.

2 Precut a good quantity of tesserae into quarters using the nippers (*see* p.17) and remember that these are to be laid ridge-side up so as to be smooth-side up in the finished slab. Using gum arabic or wallpaper paste, stick down a single ring of

3

5

4

6

5 Pour the cement into the frame until it is half full. Using snips, cut a square of chicken wire and place this into the frame, then sandwich it in with another layer of cement until the frame is full. Smooth the surface using a trowel. Cover the frame with plastic sheeting and leave to dry for a week.

6 To unmould the slab, remove all the screws. Tap the battens until they fall away. Pull the cement slab and the board apart; the paper should come away with the board, exposing the mosaic surface. If a few tesserae remain stuck to the paper, these can be refixed with grout. Vacuum or sweep the sand off the mosaic, stick any missing tesserae back in and allow them to dry for an hour. Polish the surface of the slab with a stiff household brush or non-metal kitchen scourer and grout in the usual manner (*see* p.17).

dark tesserae to establish the border, then work area by area, 'nibbling' the quarters into triangles with the nippers to accommodate diagonal lines. Leave small gaps between the tesserae for grouting. The introduction of even darker tesserae into the dark areas will give the piece depth of tone and introduce an interesting 'flicker'

effect. Keeping the tesserae even and rectilinear across the piece (*see* pp.20–21), fill the whole design with vitreous glass.

3 Saw the wooden battens into short sections and place these around the edge of the mosaic surface, leaving only a 2mm (¹⁄₁₆in) gap. Screw the adjoining battens to each other and also to

the base board. Brush petroleum jelly over the inner side of the resulting frame (to act as a 'release' agent), but avoid getting it on the tesserae. Sprinkle fine sand into the frame and brush it around with an artist's paintbrush so that it fills all the crevices.

4 Wearing rubber gloves, mix three parts of sand to one part of cement; make a well in the centre and add water until the consistency is like that of wet mud.

LAYING MOSAIC TESSERAE

It goes without saying that the tesserae that comprise a mosaic work must be arranged in *some* order, even if this order is a random one. By virtue of the nature of the medium, the mosaicist must think not only about the materials, motifs and colours to be used, but equally about how the individual tesserae are to be juxtaposed. The possibilities are endless, the choices made depending upon the shape of the tesserae, their depth and scale, and a large number of aesthetic factors, such as how closely packed the tesserae are, the nature of the spaces (or interstices) left between them, whether they align or misalign, are set in distinct rows or 'jigsawed' together in a 'crazy paved' arrangement.

There are today no strict rules determining how tesserae should be laid, but conventions have grown up over centuries that offer a reliable route to practical and/or expressive results. Largely as a consequence of their ability to cut stone to a specific shape and size, the Romans developed certain classic setting patterns which they codified with such names as '*opus vermiculatum*' and '*opus tessellatum*' and employed systematically to great artistic effect.

The motif of the dog (opposite, top right) is surrounded by a sort of halation of white marble consisting of a double row of outlining tesserae. *Vermis* is Latin for worm, and in '*opus vermiculatum*' the background literally worms around the motif, providing emphasis. More than two or three rows of this effect might, however, make it appear over-prominent, so the bulk of the background in this example is infilled with '*opus tessellatum*', a rectilinear arrangement of small cubic tesserae. The mosaicist has carefully negotiated the meeting of these two setting conventions, using smaller,

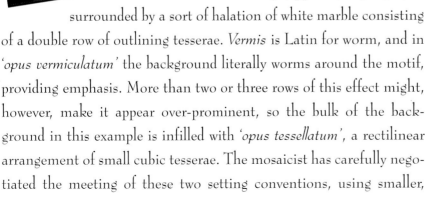

This panel from Martin Cheek's Punch Flip *sequence (left) is a joyous example of a modern work in which lines of setting are all-important to convey movement. The smalti used for Mr Punch's body run longitudinally, like the stripes on his tunic, and are made more emphatic because they are ungrouted. These lines are gently echoed by those in the vitreous glass background, which, though more random, flow in response to the shape and action of the figure.*

Modern mosaic owes a great deal to the eloquent settings employed by Byzantine mosaicists (see pp.8–9), who excelled in describing form through contour. The head of Empress Theodora from San Vitale in Ravenna (right) is an accomplished feat of portraiture largely because of the way in which the various shapes and intricate arrangement of the tesserae describe the modelling and texture of the face.

The famous Roman threshold sign warning of the presence of a dog (far right, top) shows the combined use of two standard Roman setting techniques, opus vermiculatum and opus tessellatum.

But the Romans didn't confine themselves solely to opus tessellatum for their backgrounds, and explored a wide range of different setting patterns, including fan or scalework arrangements (far right, below).

tapered pieces of marble to fill any irregular spaces that occur. This setting combination may be found in a huge number of Roman mosaics.

Byzantine mosaicists, fascinated by the description of form in glass and stone, used lines of setting almost like broad, curved brushstrokes to establish the contours of faces and drapery (*see* caption).

The modern objective is usually to achieve powerful and expressive settings, and although this is realized in a wide variety of different ways, mosaicists tend to lay the most emphatic lines first to establish the physical and emotive structure of their subject followed by any secondary figures in the design and, finally, the background.

OBJECTS
Bits and Pieces

❖

TABLES

FRAMES AND
MIRRORS

CONTAINERS

JEWELLERY

Portable mosaic objects offer an excellent way of enjoying the beauty of the medium without having to commit to architectural permanence. Pieces can be combined and contrasted to establish a mosaic *leitmotiv* within a room, ranging from the smallest articles, such as delicate boxes, to large items of furniture. Nor need such objects be entirely functional; many artists sculpt with mosaic or produce distinctive jewellery from tiny tesserae.

❖

Tabletops provide an exciting 'canvas' on which the imagination may have free rein. The tesserae should create a flush surface and be grouted for the sake of practicality, but there are no restrictions upon the colours and forms used, as is exuberantly demonstrated by this bold, abstract design in smashed ceramic.

OBJECTS: BITS AND PIECES

For hundreds of years mosaic has been used to decorate objects, in addition to walls and pavements, since it offers the compelling benefit of a concealing shell that can transform the plain, the ordinary and the mundane into the opulent, the rich and the jewelled. No special moulds or cumbersome equipment are required – simply patience and skill – so mosaic decoration is also recommended by a lack of technical complexity. The variety of possible applications is as multifarious as the objects to which mosaic may be applied, and it will adhere equally well to most solid materials: wood, metal, ceramic and plastic being the most usual bases.

Once encrusted with mosaic a mass-produced item immediately becomes a unique object, a highly gratifying transformation which, depending upon the scale of the work, may be effected within a single day. Thus objects quickly take on the presence of sculptures, their forms being made more eloquent through their interpretation in mosaic: an ordinary frying pan becomes a quasi-tribal wall-plaque (left) and a dresser plays a game of *trompe l'oeil* with the viewer (right) – two quite different treatments, both of which offer a jokey reformulation of the original and unexcitingly familiar object.

Such objects may be functional or purely decorative, from furniture to sculpture, from jewellery to items that lose their practicality precisely because mosaic has been applied to them. In each case the interest lies as much in the mosaicist's adaptation as in the beauty or character of the finished piece of work.

Objects are excellent subjects for new mosaicists as the scale and complexity of each project undertaken may be closely controlled. A complete beginner might start with something that is regular and flat,

Cleo Mussi's Red Tailed Monkey with Green Sideboards *(left) is a wonderfully quirky interpretation of an ordinary frying pan and has something of the same witty brutalism as Picasso's surreal reworkings of everyday objects.*

Whereas Cleo Mussi's frying pan (opposite) is deliberately rendered non-functional, the dresser (left) is playfully self-referential to its function. Smashed dinner plates have been carefully pieced back together and are ranged along the shelves, parodying the standard method of display. This mosaic trompe-l'oeil effect is just one of the many visual puns that may be executed in the medium.

such as a mirror surround (*see* pp.42–3), or that does not take long to complete, such as small-scale jewellery (*see* pp.52–3 and 54–5). The former will not present the problem of sharp edges appearing proud of the mosaic surface, whilst the latter does not represent an enormous investment if the first attempt is not a resounding success.

For the more experienced mosaicist there are appropriate challenges, too, such as how to maintain the utility of an object that, for instance, has to be resistant to water or else needs some other special treatment to suit it to its intended function. The shapes undertaken and the materials applied can also become more complex and with time the

decorator of a small rectilinear box with a simple motif in vitreous glass tesserae may graduate to become the designer of a large curvaceous sculptural object embellished with tesserae in a range of different materials.

Above all, objects offer an unparalleled opportunity for self-expression. They allow the mosaicist freely to experiment with the juxtapositions of mixed media, to design objects utterly to their own specification and of their own invention, and to

Rebecca Newnham has used mirror glass to create these striking shoe sculptures (above), which have no purpose but to be sensual objects of fascination, quintessentially glamorous and impractical. Mosaic is, on the other hand, only one element in Heather Burrell's functional Baroness Mosaic Chair *(opposite), its vibrancy and 'patchwork' pattern contrasting with the monochrome metal wrought in torturous arabesques.*

recycle and revamp those things with which they have become over-familiar.

This innate adaptability also makes objects in mosaic highly saleable as they are generally able to fit into most interiors or exteriors with ease. A chair, a dresser or a mirror are far more readily assimilable into most homes than a mosaic floor slab or wall plaque, both of which are likely to require pre-planning when the room is decorated.

Mosaic objects also make exceptional gifts, in that they are both personal and thoughtful but do not commit the recipient to make any radical changes to accommodate them. Whilst being original works of art they may be sat upon, poured from and looked in, have things stored in them, or displayed upon them. Drawing inspiration from the Surrealists, the inventive mosaicist can play with the visual possibilities inherent in objects themselves: a table could be interpreted as a four-legged animal; earrings fashioned in the form of ears; or a mirror decorated with a face.

Happily, a reasonable number of mosaic artefacts have survived the centuries to offer inspiration today. For hundreds of years the medium has been used to embellish ritual objects, the most famous example of this being the fabulous productions of the Mayas and Aztecs. Continuing a long tradition of mosaic art in pre-Columbian America, these civilizations used turquoise and jade to adorn objects such as shields, knives and masks; indeed, the Aztec king, Montezuma II, presented Cortés, the Spanish conqueror of Mexico, with a number of mosaic masks believed to avert evil.

TABLES

Tables offer the mosaicist an excellent opportunity to work on a medium-sized independent project and they are extremely flexible in terms of the styles and extent of the decoration that may be applied to them. Each affords a tempting blank canvas in the form of a flat, level tabletop. Methods of application can vary, but the main challenge is the creation of a smooth, practical surface. Many may also benefit from mosaic being applied to their other surfaces.

The enormous variety of types and purposes of table means that there is vast scope in terms of the shape and size of the basic object; but unless mosaic is to be applied very sparingly, there is little point in investing in an expensive item – the table need only be sound and suitable for your purposes. It is important, however, that these purposes be clearly established from the outset, because function and siting will dictate the materials that may be used.

Metal bases are undoubtedly preferable to wood for tables sited outdoors as they have a greater resilience to damp conditions, but it is essential that the metal is sealed in order to retard corrosion and to make its surface receptive to adhesive. Ornamented metal-based tables should not be left out in extremes of temperature because the mobility of the metal may cause the mosaic cladding to crack and break off; the thicker the base, the fewer problems there will be in this area. PVA adhesive will not be sufficient for works sited outdoors, so choose instead a strong cement-based adhesive (*see* pp.14–15) suitable for

The wit of this small piece (left) resides in the fact that not only is every surface of the table infested with mosaic, but it has also crept up over the flower vase. Thus the mosaic cladding becomes a surreal camouflage, making a bizarre 'twinset' out of two quite distinct objects. This somewhat arch treatment is in keeping with the pseudo-genteel style of the table and the squat, domestic shape of the vase, both of which are simultaneously parodied and elevated by their new mosaic skin. Crockery has been set into a thick grey grout so that the vase resembles a piece of cloisonné enamel.

This Tartan Tabletop (below) by Emma Biggs of Mosaic Workshop (see also pp.42–3, 54–5 and 74–5) uses the conceit of a crumpled, checked fabric to create a fascinating abstract pattern that also resembles an aerial photograph of a landscape.

In her Gaming Table (right) Zoë Candlin incorporates chess and backgammon boards. These are both a practical feature of the table and the pivot for its design. In creating a gaming table Zoë (see also pp.32–7) continues a long tradition, but in employing mosaic she digresses from the materials that conventionally have been used.

bonding the tesserae to metal and a water-resistant grout intended for outdoor use. For permanent or near-permanent siting outdoors, concrete provides an excellent, inert base to which mosaic tesserae will readily adhere (*see* pp.108–11).

Round or oval tables present the mosaicist with the challenge of describing curves, a task that is most easily achieved if irregular tesserae are laid in a jigsaw-like arrangement. This type of setting is suitable for use outdoors only if the shards of ceramic or glass are of equal thickness and will lie comfortably in a plane; if they do not, the table will be more vulnerable to weather damage. Frost is particularly dangerous: moisture gets between the tesserae or into them, if porous, and expands as it freezes, causing cracking. The resulting surface must be grouted copiously to fill the interstices and cover any rough edges that may snag clothes.

When applying mosaic to tables that will be sited indoors, the mosaicist may use a far wider range of materials and techniques. PVA adhesive or tile adhesive (*see* pp.14–15) will adequately affix tesserae to wooden bases, and the wood is unlikely to need treatment, bar sealing, unless it is unsound or has been painted, waxed or varnished (in which case, such layers should be stripped). Practicality obviously has some bearing on the surfaces created, but textural effects and intricate detailing become far more feasible. The main criteria determining the nature of the mosaic decoration are therefore aesthetic rather than pragmatic.

A heavy wooden scrub table, for example, would doubtless look ludicrous if applied with a filigree of tiny glass tesserae; large, bold shards of shattered ceramic would be a far more appropriate addition. On the other hand, a modern wrought-iron table with fine curlicue legs might well invite mosaic with tesserae so fine that the effect is almost like that of inlaid marble. It is possible to apply mosaic in a way that is interestingly at odds with the character of the table, but this is an approach that can lead to some expensive mistakes. The key, therefore, is to plan ahead, use tear sheets and other visual sources for inspiration, draw designs and even scale traces that will help to anticipate the final effect.

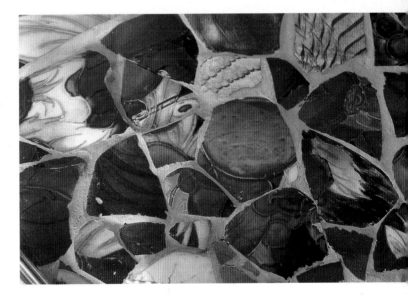

This substantial garden table (left) provides an excellent support for a smooth veneer of smashed ceramic tiles. The striking colour combinations used compensate for the lack of texture, which has been sacrificed for reasons of practicality. The kaleidoscope of ceramic shards (above) has been thickly grouted to ensure that the surface is impermeable to water and smooth to the touch.

JAZZY ABSTRACT TABLETOP

Different demands and materials require flexible practical approaches. The semi-indirect technique, which this fine tabletop demonstrates, is especially appropriate for tiles which can only be 'read' from one side and therefore cannot be placed face down using the indirect method (see pp.18–19). Zoë Candlin of After Noah views her work as ceramic collages, which often need to be adjusted and balanced as they progress, so the direct method (see pp.16–17) would also be inappropriate since it would not allow her the freedom to make changes to sections already cut and put in position. When using this semi-indirect method, however, it is essential to work on a steady surface so that individual tesserae that have been laid in place are not jolted out of alignment.

Zoë has used ordinary white household tiles, but has painted and fired them herself to create unique patterns and textures in a variety of colours. If you do not have access to a kiln, a similar effect may be achieved using an assortment of ready-made patterned tiles. Ends of lines can often be purchased extremely cheaply, so it is always worth enquiring about these. If, however, you decide to use older, non-standard tiles to cover a regular surface, like a table, do check that they are of even thickness, otherwise undesirable ridges will occur, which will be impractical and difficult to clean.

This circular tabletop has been placed on the metal base of a reproduction Victorian garden table. Such bases can be quite expensive, so it is wise to hunt around in junk shops for something suitable. Alternatively, you can make your own wooden base if you are on a tight budget.

This stunning tabletop (previous pages) is a wonderful mixture of exuberance and restraint, its vibrant polychrome border being firmly held in check by a cool white centre.

Materials
Table base
Medium density fibreboard (MDF) or plyboard, circular, 76cm (30in) in diameter
White paper
Tracing paper
Ceramic tiles
Wallpaper paste
Pattern paper
Waterproof tile cement and spreader
Grout
Flexible metal edging strip and nails

Tools
Pencil
Tile cutter
Nippers
Household paintbrush
Scalpel
Lint-free cloth
Rolling pin
Sponge

1

1 Consider carefully the sort of design that will suit the base and work out in advance the range of colours and patterns you intend to use. Once these broad parameters have been established, either sketch the design directly on to the fibreboard or plyboard or else first work it out on paper and trace it down on to the board. Don't draw in every tessera; a broad pattern will suffice as a guide as it is important to allow leeway for improvisation when the tiles are being laid in position.

2

2 Trim away the curved edges of each tile with the cutter by scoring along all four sides and snapping them off. Cut the remaining piece into four or five strips, again using the cutter, and either leave these strips intact or cut them with the nippers into roughly square tesserae (*see* p.17). You may, of course, cut the tiles into any shape you require using a combination of the cutter and nippers. Zoë has used triangles and large squares as well as strips and more standard rectangular shapes.

3

4

5

3 Start to lay the mosaic from the centre outwards, aligning the white tesserae in a single direction. Where these regular lines meet the curve of the border it is advisable to lay a row of white or coloured tesserae to describe the curve, then cut those tesserae at the edge of the straight rows neatly to fill any irregular spaces. The curve of the border may be achieved by very slightly tapering the tesserae with the nippers. None should overhang the edges of the tabletop as this will make it impossible to attach an edging strip. Don't precut all the tiles you will use as you are likely to want to match, contrast and tailor some pieces whilst you work. Once the entire area of the board is covered and you have made any last-minute revisions to the design, cut a piece of strong yet thin paper (layout, pattern or photocopy paper is ideal) and brush one side of it with a thick solution of wallpaper paste. Lift this soggy sheet and very carefully lay it paste-side down over the surface of the tesserae. Should wrinkles occur, don't try to lift and relay it; simply smooth down the folds and pass a rolling pin over the surface to encourage adhesion. If there are any parts that have not adhered, make a tiny hole in the paper and insert some more paste through it, or if the paper has not adequately covered the whole area, cut another piece large enough to overlap with that already laid. Roughly trim off any excess and leave to dry overnight.

4 Preferably with the help of a second person, lift the paper and attached tesserae off the board and on to another flat, clean surface. If the paper is likely to tear when carried in one piece, use a scalpel to divide it into jagged sections that may be moved independently then reassembled like a jigsaw.

6

5 Prepare the surface of the board with an even coating of waterproof tile cement, which is best applied with a spreader. Once the entire surface has been covered, carefully lower the paper tesserae-side down on to the board and check the edges for overhang. If this has occurred, adjust the position of the paper very slightly using both hands. This stage is very tricky – too much movement will make the tiles slide and overlap, so it really helps to have an assistant here.

6 Once the tesserae have been evenly and firmly pressed into the cement, dampen the paper with a wet sponge and gently peel it back to reveal the mosaic surface. Wipe off excess glue or paper with a damp lint-free cloth and allow any moisture to evaporate. It is important to check all the tiles are in place and not overhanging before the cement dries. If there are still any overhanging tesserae, carefully trim them back using the nippers. Once you are entirely happy with the surface, leave to dry for 24 hours (or as instructed on the cement container), then grout in the normal manner (*see* p.17). Finally, apply the flexible edging strip, securing it into the board with nails. Clean off any remaining glue or paper.

FRAMES AND MIRRORS

Mosaic border designs have been in existence for as long as mosaic, used as a device for defining and beautifying the edges of a work (*see* pp.112–123). By the eighteenth century they were often intricate and richly coloured and had begun to bear a distinct resemblance to ornate painted frames, although most small-scale works were usually then inserted within a gilt frame.

Nineteenth-century artists and designers, prompted by the renewed interest in craft, were increasingly experimental in their framing of paintings and objects, often making the frame part of the artwork itself. This departure from the standard gilt frame formula allowed for the introduction of new elements, including applied decoration such as mosaic.

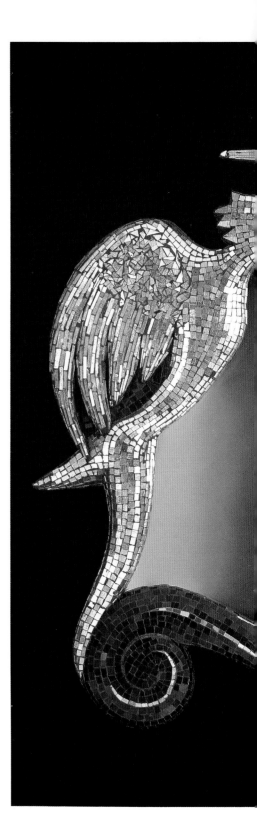

Our own century has seen an explosion of creativity in the design of both frames and mirror surrounds, which are now made from an incredible number of different materials – from plastic to papier mâché. In this climate of experimentation mosaic is the perfect medium, combining diversity with versatility to allow works to be custom-made, each one having a unique and unrepeatable arrangement of tesserae even if its base object is mass-produced.

For this reason many people choose to buy ready-made mirrors and frames that they then disguise with mosaic. This is a perfectly valid approach (*see* pp.40–1), but it can be exciting to design the base object too (*see* above left and right). Mirrored glass itself can add an extra dimension to decorated mirrors. Cut into tesserae it can be used to create reflective surrounds for smooth mirror. Alternatively, mirror tesserae can be pieced together to create a whole, fragmented, mirror.

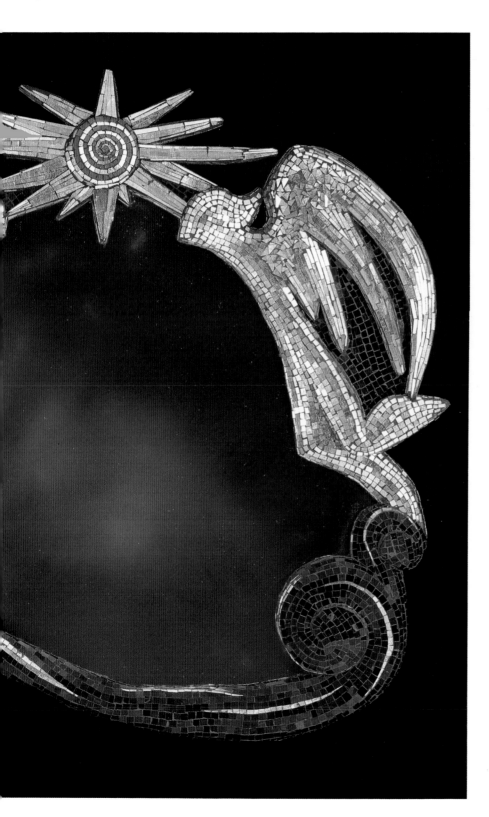

The sea horse (opposite) is, strictly speaking, neither a mirror nor a frame, but a decorative wall mosaic playing with mirrored surfaces that would be particularly suitable for a bathroom. In concept and execution it is extremely straightforward: an outline motif is chosen (see pp.112–123), traced on to a piece of medium density fibreboard (MDF) or plyboard and cut out with a jigsaw; the details of the design are then sketched directly on to the board to offer a guide for the placing of the gold and silver smalti and/or mirror glass, which is cut with nippers into regular rectangular strips. These tesserae are then laid over beads of PVA adhesive, packed tightly together in neat courses that alleviate the need for grouting. In this way one might easily create a series of different sea creatures which, if sited around a bathroom, would make a satisfying and unified scheme.

Rebecca Newnham's fantastical mirror, Icarus and Daedalus, (left) is a sculptural cartouche infused with wit and imagination. The two strangely proportioned mythological figures are borne up out of a sweeping blue scroll in a manner obliquely reminiscent of Botticelli's Birth of Venus and, in accordance with the near-symmetry on which the whole design pivots, they match but are subtly different. Mirror glass is used throughout to extend the reflectivity of the central mirror across the entire object and colour is exploited to give the piece depth, energy and, with the use of dark blue, a firm horizontal anchor. The object is an inspired blend of reference and innovation – a true work of mosaic art.

The standard square picture frame offers a perfect testing ground for the creation of particular moods and effects through mosaic. Within the microcosm of the encircling border, combinations of colour and texture may be explored and unusual elements introduced. The mosaicist may wish to stress the relationship to the image framed, and collage, but also pays homage to such artists as Duchamp and to Picasso's reworkings of the 'found' object. In these days of environmental awareness, most references of this sort will also be read in the light of recycling, an interesting second layer of meaning that can only contribute to the dialogue between image and frame.

therefore employ mosaic 'ingredients' that are keyed to its subject matter. An old photograph might benefit from being juxtaposed with fragments of contemporary objects, such as antique buttons, or a seaside snap from the proximity of pebbles and shells (see above centre). This sort of themed response is akin to the conventions of

But such references are not obligatory – indeed, they limit future uses of the frame – and the work may equally well be completely abstract, composed of tesserae that have no meaning beyond their aesthetic impact when used in combination. It is always important for the mosaicist to keep these combinations in control by making conscious choices about what to include and what to exclude. A completely random medley of tesserae of all shapes, sizes, hues, textures and materials *may* be effective, but will be so only by fluke, whereas a more limited 'palette' is likely to pack a far stronger visual and emotional punch. This is not to say that all hues must be harmonious and all textures

The exquisite bathroom mirror (below left) by Candace Bahouth (see also pp.40, 80–1, 84 and 108–11) is a harmonious symphony in blues, with purple and turquoise 'bands' sandwiching a layer of elegant Chinese crockery. The use of unusual pink grout endows the work with playfulness, vibrancy and vigour.

The photo frame (below centre) is a

homogenous, but rather to suggest that the effects, whether they arise from contrast or similarity, be anticipated and controlled.

If the technical challenges posed by covering a frame in mosaic are few, the artistic ones are mani-fold, and for this reason such projects are excellent for the new mosaicist (*see* pp.42–3).

mosaic still-life of small objects found on the beach, including shells, stones and pieces of smoothed glass. The yellowy-orange-coloured grout suggests that these objects remain embedded in sand.

The bejewelled frame (above) is unashamedly over the top for which reason the image it frames is intentionally sparse, restrained and colourless, a dramatic 'role reversal'.

MEXICAN TERRACOTTA MIRROR

This radiating mirror surround, though simple in design, is astonishingly striking and evocative. Emma Biggs of Mosaic Workshop (*see* also pp.28, 54–5 and 74–5) has exclusively used Mexican ceramic tiles that are made of a matt, biscuity terracotta glazed on one side with a vibrant turquoise blue. In using these alone she creates a pleasingly homogenous effect that is yet based on variety because the texture of the rough terracotta could not be more in contrast with the smooth glaze.

The decorative conceit used is an ancient one – a simple geometric chequerboard pattern – but Emma literally puts a spin on it by describing a circular form. The effect is immediate and dramatic and draws the attention inwards, focusing it on the mirrored centre, which is thus made as prominent as the bull's-eye in a target.

The colours too have a distinct optical dynamic. Blue and orange are opposing and therefore complementary colours. Complementaries tend to be extremely satisfying when juxtaposed, and the combination is particularly successful here in creating a mood redolent of a hot, sun-parched landscape, an 'ethnic' effect enhanced by the rough, intentionally uneven texture of this ungrouted work.

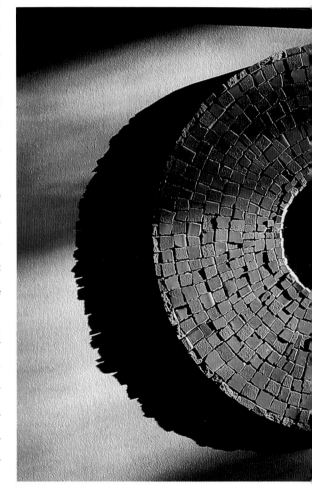

Materials	Tools
Sealed medium density	*Pencil*
fibreboard (MDF)	*Ruler*
or plyboard, 45cm	*Trowel*
(17³/₄in) diameter	*Nippers*
Precut mirror, 17cm	*Bowl*
(6³/₄in) diameter	
Silicone sealant	
20 blue-glazed	
terracotta tiles	
Latex additive adhesive	
Cement-based adhesive	
Mirror plates for	
hanging	
Screws	

1 Draw lines to establish the centre of the board and stick the mirror on to it with silicone sealant spread thinly and evenly with a trowel. Using nippers, start to cut the tiles into tesserae by halving them repeatedly (*see* p.17). Try to make the pieces as regular as possible, but don't worry if the fractures

1

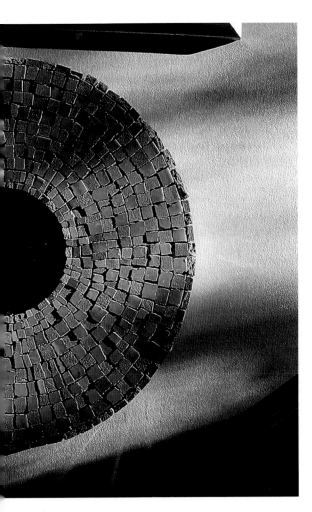

tesserae as you work in towards the centre. If you find that the pattern is going out, cheat a little by omitting a tessera – this is very unlikely to be noticeable.

3 Use the same adhesive mixture to apply alternating tesserae around the edge of the piece, 'nibbled' to the depth of the board. The glaze is likely to adhere less easily than the terracotta surface so you may either thicken up the adhesive or stick all the edging tesserae glaze-side out. Apply only as much adhesive as you will be able to cover relatively quickly.

4 Now apply tesserae with silicone sealant to cover what is known as the 'grinning edge' of the mirror. These should be cut to align with the innermost circle of the surrounding tesserae, but should be 'nibbled' to half their depth to allow them to lie flush with the rest of the mosaic surface. Let the piece dry for an hour, polish the mirror and fix mirror plates to the back of the board to hang it.

are not straight, the glaze shatters or if there is a lot of 'crumble' and dust. Cut those tesserae that are to be blue glaze-side up, and the rest terracotta-side up. This gives a better chance of producing regular shapes.

2 Mix a small quantity of latex adhesive with an equal amount of water, then add dry cement-based adhesive, blending it all to the consistency of a stiff cake mixture. Starting at the outer edge of the board, spread the resulting adhesive quite thickly on to a small segment and start sticking down the tesserae, working inwards row-by-row in concentric circles. Use smaller

CONTAINERS

The category of containers embraces an enormous range of diverse objects – from boxes and bowls to goblets and vases – all of which can provide challenging bases for mosaic. Little is more satisfying than effecting the complete transformation of something mundane and particular pleasure may be derived from reclothing humdrum pieces in fabulous vestments of vivid tesserae.

At the outset of each project a basic decision must be made about whether it should remain functional. With a box the answer is likely to be that it should because the inside will be mosaic-free and the outside can generally be designed to allow for opening and closure, but with a goblet, for example, the function of the object may well have to be sacrificed – if clad with mosaic it will tend to be rather uncomfortable to hold, prone to damage and difficult to wash (*see* right).

This decision profoundly affects the choice of objects to be decorated, the type of decoration applied and the materials used in the process. Advice cannot be given for all eventualities, but the main practical hazards are damp and water damage, and wear and tear. If the object is to remain functional, protect it from the former by sealing the base, using a water-resistant cement tile adhesive (*see* pp.14–15) and ensure that the tesserae are impervious. However, to protect any mosaic object against everyday wear and tear is more difficult, but the aim should be to make the surface of the tesserae as smooth and seamless as possible and to ensure that they are firmly and securely embedded in the cement and/or grout.

Once these practical parameters have been worked out, enormous fun may be had with the object. If it is small then there is a greater likelihood that 'choice' tesserae may be used throughout; if large, then

Rebecca Newnham's goblets (below) are intentionally non-functional, as is obvious from their crenellated rims. Like medieval chalices, their bodies – made of silver, brass and copper – have been designed to be both decorative in themselves and to receive ornamentation; these are works distinctly indebted to the magnificence of ecclesiastical plate, but equally to Gothic design, fairy stories and even the iconology of chess. This variety of sources makes it all the more appropriate that the mosaic tesserae should also be of mixed inspiration: 2mm-thick glass that has been applied with gold and silver leaf to resemble precious metal.

The exterior of this classically-shaped urn (right) is entirely covered with a miscellany of smashed crockery and tiles that have been applied as rough, uneven lozenges. This pleasing restlessness – the tesserae appear to be jostling for position – is reinforced by the 'colour rhythm' of the piece, the blues and greens that form the base colouring being punctuated by a scattering of contrasting primaries.

the piece can offer scope for unconventional design solutions and representational depictions. It is also interesting to 'makeover' a number of identical bases in totally different ways in order to experiment with a range of distinct effects. Whilst one terracotta jar might be roughly coated with multi-coloured smashed ceramic (*see* above), a second could be clad with a harmonious palette of quartered vitreous glass tesserae and a third with 'found' objects, such as buttons and even badges. When making mosaic containers as gifts or for sale, do remember to offer guidelines about the care they require and any safety instructions, especially if children are likely to handle them.

INTRICATE OCTOPUS CASKET

Stephen Windsor Clive is a proponent of authentic mosaic as opposed to what he terms 'tiny tiling'. He tries always to use smalti, marble and pebbles in preference to vitreous glass tesserae or smashed crockery, and to adhere to original methods of application, particularly those practised by the Romans.

The principle or meaning of authentic mosaic is the random, organic and seemlessly flowing effect that is achieved by hand-placing the tesserae. In this, his workshop is steadfast

and, when possible, uses the large slabs of smalti that arrive directly from Venice as well as copying and adapting original historical designs. His work therefore runs the gamut from direct 'facsimile' reproductions, through interpretations and adaptations, to new, unique works, such as the encrusted steel casket demonstrated here. Nor is Stephen afraid to borrow from more recent sources, his liberal tastes ranging from nineteenth-century pattern books to Islamic art and the work of twentieth-century designers. All Stephen's projects – from grottoes (*see* pp.94–5) to jewellery – are executed according to a firm belief in the importance of simple decorative mosaic, free from unnecessary gimmicks and conceits; he even eschews the use of grout, preferring that the lines of setting be pronounced and unmodified.

The tesserae suggested for use here are those of Stephen's preference and recommendable if they are readily available. If not, the piece may be completed using vitreous glass, although the texture achieved maybe less choppy and exciting.

This magnificent octopus casket (left) revels in the rich, strong colours of Venetian smalti, which afford it a satisfyingly irregular and highly reflective surface.

Because the lid of the box (far left) does not describe the entire beast, it looks almost abstract in design, the octopus's body being made up of greens and browns, purple, black, grey and even crimson.

This close-up detail (above) of the facing side of the box shows how strongly the lines of setting appear when smalti is left ungrouted (see pp.20–21).

1

2

Materials
Metal box or casket,
*   approximately*
*   30 x 20 x 20cm*
*   (12 x 8 x 8in)*
Epoxy resin adhesive
Sand
Uncut or cut marble
Uncut or cut smalti
White cement
Lime
Hydrochloric acid

Tools
Small mixing bowl
Spatula
Sieve
Ruler or tape measure
Pen
Tracing paper
Scissors
Hammer and hardie
Ink pen
Rubber gloves
Toothbrush

1 Mix a small bowl of epoxy resin according to the proportions specified on the container: usually five of resin to one of hardener. Apply this mixture to one side of the box, spreading it thinly and evenly with a spatula, then sieve some dry sand and sprinkle this over the resin so as completely to cover it. Shake off the excess and repeat this process on each side.

2 Draw the dimensions of the five sides of the box on to tracing paper. Choose a motif that can extend across all the sides (*see* pp.112–123) and sketch in its basic outlines. Cut out this trace and wrap it round the box to check that the design is satisfactory when viewed from all angles.

3 In a small bowl mix one part each of white cement, lime and sand with water to a buttery consistency, sufficient to cover one side of the box. Apply this with a spatula and smooth it down flush with the rim.

4 Ink in the corresponding part of the design trace and press it down on to the surface so as to leave an impression of the motif on the wet cement.

5 Break up sufficient tesserae to cover one side of the box (this may be done in advance). Stephen uses blocks of marble and uncut smalti broken with a hammer and hardie to a roughly even size and depth (*see* pp.12–13), but if unable to obtain these materials and tools, precut smalti or marble may be

3

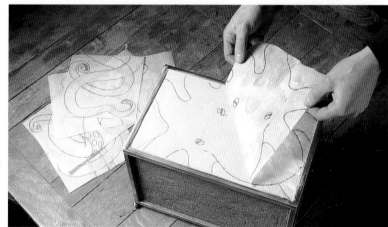

4

substituted, as may vitreous glass tesserae that can be cut with nippers. When marble slabs are cut, the non-polished (or inside) surface is normally used in mosaic.

Working inwards from the edge, press the tesserae firmly into the cement with your fingers, following the inked design as a guide. Once one side has been completed, start to apply cement and tesserae to the next until the box is entirely covered. Leave to dry for two or three days then, wearing rubber gloves, scrub the surface with a toothbrush and wipe it with a weak dilute solution of hydrochloric acid (*see* pp.14–15) to clear any stray cement.

5

JEWELLERY

There is a natural affinity between mosaic and jewellery because precious and semi-precious gems have been used in mosaic works for hundreds of years. The techniques too are complementary because both gems and tesserae are set into a base to form a decorative and light-reflective surface. The main differences between the jeweller's craft and that of the mosaicist have therefore been to do with scale and the use of precious metals. In one of his most intricate masterpieces, the *Imperial Mosaic Egg* of 1914, the great Russian jeweller Peter Carl Fabergé was, however, able to realize a fabulous fusion of the two art forms, albeit on a small scale, by setting tiny tesserae of precious gems within an exceptionally fine metal mesh.

The explosion of costume jewellery since the late Victorian period has increasingly freed jewellers to use unorthodox and non-precious materials, including paste, plastic, putty, paint, paper, glass and base metals, a development that has made mosaic an ideal medium for jewellery. For a small expenditure on materials and in a relatively short space of time even a beginner may produce distinctive mosaic objects that have all the sparkle and glamour of real jewellery without the costs and risks involved in wearing it. Indeed, mosaic earrings, brooches, necklaces and even rings can be more striking and fun to wear than their 'real' counterparts, which are understandably constrained by gem sizes and setting conventions.

To produce successful mosaic jewellery one must obviously have a certain manual dexterity and the ability to keep a close eye on the weight and balance of the work, but the key to the creation of objects that beg to be worn is imagination and the ability to imbue each piece with character and charm.

This small camel necklace by Andrew Logan (far left) is in effect a tiny sculpture suspended from a chain. Small, irregular shards of mirror glass create a glistening, almost reptilian skin on the body of the beast, contrasting dramatically with the texture and colour of its appealing faux gem burden.

The stunning collection of jewellery by Ray Halsall (left) demonstrates the splendours that may be achieved when wit, imagination and dexterity combine in a single mosaicist's work (see also pp.52–3). Mirror glass, faux gems and glitter are Ray's basic materials, but they assume quite different appearances within an enormously varied repertoire that extends from relatively discreet stud earrings to extravagant necklaces that are themselves composites of smaller mosaic elements.

Julie Arkell's Papier-Mâché Dog (above) is a mosaic mongrel of smashed crockery, coloured glass, mirror glass, faux gems and pearls. Its naïve shape, flattened to two dimensions, endows it with a beguiling appearance, but also makes for a more easily decorated surface. The papier-mâché base has been completely disguised by a thick, even layer of gold paint to resemble metal.

GLITZY GLAMOUR EARRINGS

Ray Halsall's creations are not for the demure or retiring. Fashioned from broken mirror, *faux* gems and glitter, they are an inspired blend of art deco, punk and '90s style, redolent of the decadence and the hedonism of an unbridled nightlife. They are for sybarites, whose passions are strong and instincts bold; Baudelairian types who revel in the sumptuous and the exotic.

When the wearer of these earrings turns her head, she will scatter a shower of dancing lights about her, a modern nimbus that has little to do with religion and everything to do with attraction, for these are seductresses' earrings, inviting attention with their movement, sparkle and passionate blood-red centres.

Though easy and quick to make, and of materials that cost next to nothing, these earrings are both classy and dressy. On their own they are enough to turn the famous 'little black dress' into an outfit; one that pays homage to Hollywood and at the same time to the fabulous excesses of Glam Rock. But this is not to say that this jewellery is vulgar – far from it; for its one-off, home-made quality imbues it with a delicacy and sensitivity far from the smooth, impersonal sheen of mass-produced costume jewellery.

These drop earrings are, of course, just one of the many shapes and types of jewellery that may be created using Ray's versatile technique. With the appropriate findings and settings, it is equally easy to make brooches, pendants and rings.

Materials

Plain white paper
Acetate
Mirror glass
Two red faux *gems*
Chemical metal and
   hardener
Fine glitter
Medium thick wire

Tools

Pen
Scalpel
Glass cutter
Flat-edged pliers or
   nippers
Short mixing stick
Toothbrush

These 'neo-art-deco' drop earrings (left) are the perfect fusion of 1930s and 1990s style, combining the high glamour of mirror glass with the inspired randomness of the home-made.

1

1 Draw the basic outline of the earrings on to a piece of paper. Using a glass cutter wheel and/or pliers or nippers, cut some ordinary mirror glass into triangles that are of the same size as the pendent tears of the earrings. Also cut long mirror strips and cut these further into small squares. Fashion the triangles into tear shapes by nibbling the two lower corners into curves and cut the resulting shape into approximately six irregular pieces. For the stud sections of the earrings nibble the small squares into tiny flat-topped triangles and arrange them in circular patterns with the red *faux* gems at their centre.

3 Again working one shape at a time, mix more chemical metal and apply it liberally to the back of the shape. Press a pierced-ear pin into the centre of each of the stud pieces and embed small loops, made from medium thick wire, into all four shapes so that the stud and pendent part of each earring may be joined together. Wet your finger slightly and draw the still-malleable chemical metal up and over these attachments to embed them securely. Glitter and/or sequins may then be applied over the surface as in step 2. Once all the pieces have dried, polish them with a soft toothbrush.

3

2 Draw the outlines again on to a second piece of paper and cover this with a thin acetate sheet. Mix the chemical metal with hardener in the proportions specified on the tube and apply it very thickly on to the acetate within the contour of one of the tear shapes. The chemical metal dries so quickly that only one shape may be attempted at a time. (The following process is the same for each of the four shapes.) Using a scalpel, rapidly transfer the mirror shards from the paper on to the surface of the chemical metal, and gently push them down into it. Once each shape is complete, bury it in a generous mound of fine glitter and leave it for about thirty seconds. Shake off the excess glitter, pat in any that seem loose, and slightly neaten the edge of the shape if necessary by gently coaxing the chemical metal with the scalpel blade. Peel the shape off the acetate.

2

DIAPHANOUS BUTTERFLY BROOCH

As demonstrated by this project and by the mirrored earrings (*see* pp.52–3), mosaic need not only be used for substantial works; it is equally well suited to delicate objects on a small scale and is now a very popular medium for fine jewellery.

Tessa Hunkin of Mosaic Workshop (*see also* pp.28, 42–3 and 74–5) is fascinated by insects which, with their naturally decorative shapes and small size, make an ideal subject for brooches. These tiny projects have all the sparkle of precious jewels, but are made of exactly the same glass as is used in large-scale mosaic works. The magic lies in cutting the tesserae into intricate, miniature shapes and aligning them in such a way as to make the interstices seem like fine veins. The work requires dexterity and practice, but the technique is beautifully simple and can eventually be carried out very rapidly. Use whichever implements will help you to handle the fiddly pieces – tweezers can be invaluable.

1

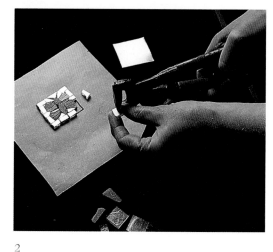

2

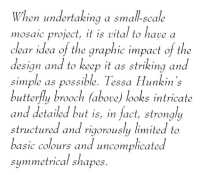

When undertaking a small-scale mosaic project, it is vital to have a clear idea of the graphic impact of the design and to keep it as striking and simple as possible. Tessa Hunkin's butterfly brooch (above) looks intricate and detailed but is, in fact, strongly structured and rigorously limited to basic colours and uncomplicated symmetrical shapes.

Materials
Brown paper
Double-sided tape
  (optional)
Silver or aluminium
  sheet
Vitreous glass and
  silver tesserae
Epoxy resin adhesive
Grout
Backing pin

Tools
Pencil and pen
Ruler
Scissors
Nippers
Lint-free cloth

1 Decide upon the dimensions of the mount and rule this area out on to a small piece of brown paper. Now clearly draw in the basic shapes of the motif and, if you feel more secure in sticking the tesserae down rather than simply laying them down loose, cover the finished design with one layer of double-sided tape. Using

3

scissors, cut the
mount out of silver or
aluminium sheet and
put it to one side.

2 Now start to cut
the tesserae to fit the
particular shapes
required by the design,
carefully 'nibbling'
them with the nippers
(*see* p.17). When
making the wings, you
may find it helpful to
cut them out as one
piece, then fracture

them to achieve the
effect of veining. As
the scale is so minute,
it is wise to have to
hand more tesserae
than you strictly need.
As you cut each piece,
lay it on the design,
sticking it to the
double-sided tape if
using. Slowly build
the image up in this
way, not worrying if
you have to take the
odd piece up to alter
its shape. Note that

the silver tesserae have
here been used silver-
side-up.

3 When all the pieces
have been cut, peel the
protective backing off
the silver or
aluminium sheet,
make sure that it is as
flat as possible and
spread the duller side
of it with an epoxy
resin. Starting at the
edges of the mosaic,
lift the tesserae piece-

by-piece off the brown
paper and place them
down in the equivalent
position on to the
silver/aluminium.
Whilst the glue is wet
there is some
flexibility in their
positioning so don't be
alarmed if at first the
fit is not so good as on
the brown paper.
Leave to dry for an
hour, then grout as
you would a larger
object (*see* p.17).

Ensure that the
surface has been wiped
absolutely clean before
the piece is left to dry
– ideally for a further
hour. Finally, attach
the backing pin with
epoxy resin.

INTERIORS
An Inside View

❖

FLOORS

WALLS

BATHROOMS

KITCHENS

Every interior in which there is mosaic decoration is unique, and it is this personal quality of the medium combined with its adaptability and beauty that make it so desirable an addition both to homes and public buildings. Stone and ceramic tesserae make practical and hard-wearing floors, walls and beautiful waterproof surfaces. Unlike much art, mosaic is both serviceable and ornamental, enlivening dull spaces with a riot of colour, pattern and rhythm that elevate an entire room.

❖

The stairwell of this modern French home invites angular, conspicuous decoration, which here takes the form of geometric mosaic designs redolent of Moresque tilework. The flooring and mosaic bannister detailing have been conceived as part of a unified scheme, which graphically illustrates how versatile and complementary mosaic can be.

INTERIORS: AN INSIDE VIEW

Mosaic has been used in interiors for thousands of years as it is one of the most durable and adaptable wall and floor coverings known to man. It is suitable for almost any space, will adhere to most surfaces, is resistant to stains, insulatory, hardwearing and rarely prone to fade. The tesserae may be applied in a regular, rectilinear arrangement or a one-off asymmetrical pattern and the design may be purely decorative or else representational, possibly with some thematic reference to the function of the room. But over and above this range of benefits and possibilities, all mosaic will lend personality to an interior, distinguishing it from others and making a visual statement, however small.

Happily, there are no aesthetic rules or conventions governing the application of mosaic. So distinctive and versatile is the medium that it exempts itself from conventions of taste, so one will find it in an enormous number of interior incarnations: in alcoves and fireplaces, as dados and borders on walls, on the risers of steps, on hearths, on working surfaces, and inset as 'rugs' and borders in floors.

Because it is so characterful, however, one must beware of mosaic 'shouting down' the other features of a room. In order to avoid this it is best either to introduce a number of related mosaic elements that balance the effect or else to key the mosaic to other objects and features that echo its colours and shapes. Even when an entire floor is covered in mosaic to which all the objects in the room are inevitably anchored, it is preferable that there should be some visual connection that will make the floor and furniture coalesce.

The fall of light – both natural and artificial – is also an essential consideration in the planning of interior schemes. On a wall beside a bright window mosaic decoration needs plenty of tonal contrast if it is

An ordinary fireplace (above left) becomes a spectacular focal point when thickly clad with a wild medley of smashed crockery.

A regular, geometric repeat design (above) allows a large expanse of wall to be covered in a way that is striking but not overbearing.

This 'crazy-paved' floor (below) is modern but reminiscent of '50s style, as are the accompanying chair and table. Chosen judiciously, furniture can be used in this way to highlight the key mood of a mosaic.

not to be erased by its *contre jour* location; it may also be appropriate to soften and diffuse the light striking a warm-coloured stone floor (see p.61) or throw a sharp and dramatic raking light on to a feature that has a particularly interesting texture. Try to avoid central lighting, as this tends to make mosaic look dull, and strip lighting, which can bleach out subtleties of tone. Remember too that the colours of light can enhance or detract. If a mosaic is to be lit primarily by artificial light, experiment with different tones to see which produce the most appealing result. A general-purpose tungsten bulb generally sheds a warm, golden glow, whereas halogen bulbs offer cooler colours.

The floor (below) blends different types of tesserae almost in the manner of a textile collage. A sense of movement is introduced through loosely directional lines of setting that establish a spiral anchored to a sequence of small round white tiles. The conceits of Synthetic Cubism might well have suggested the use of the smashed ceramic door numbers.

The wall (right) owes much to the traditions of grotto design (see pp.94–5) as it is entirely encrusted with shells. These have been laid so as to create border patterns around features and a regular infill texture that is relieved by an even scattering of larger shells. The mirror and chair have been 'keyed' into the scheme, the former by being shattered and having its edges rounded off, the

latter by emulating the shape of a shell.

The Neo-Roman marble floor (opposite) uses large expanses of opus tessellatum (see pp.20–1) that has been laid using the indirect method (see pp.18–19), as is apparent from the straight 'seams' running between the various sections. Despite these, the effect is homogenous, unified by the texture of the stone and its muted, warm colours.

There are as many possible mosaic design solutions as there are interiors, so it may be helpful to bear in mind the following considerations. Choose a design that is neither gimmicky nor likely to date and ensure that it is in proportion with the overall dimensions of the space. Suit the materials to the function and look of the room, taking into account the texture and reflectiveness of the tesserae. Satisfy yourself that the scheme will tolerate decorative changes over time and, as discussed, take lighting conditions into account. But even more importantly, have fun with the medium; stretch your imagination to the limits in the creation of a room that is quintessentially your own.

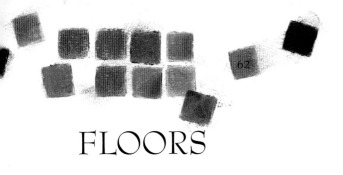

FLOORS

The Romans were great masters of mosaic flooring and ran the gamut of possible production – from small-scale works for domestic interiors to enormous pavimental mosaics for civic spaces. They developed an extensive 'grammar' of repeat geometric patterns for borders and infilled areas, which they used in conjunction with *emblemata*, intricate representational panels (*see* p.8).

The 'templates' provided by these examples are so many and so varied that Roman influence has pervaded the design of mosaic floors for hundreds of years. Because floors are a permanent feature of a room, providing its key note, they have tended to be more conserva-

The floor panel (below left) is just one of the sixty-one thematic panels that Boris Anrep designed for the National Gallery, London, between 1928 and 1952. He believed that a particularly intimate relationship is created between floor mosaics and the onlooker by virtue of their being trodden upon.

Paris Ceramics' copy of a Roman floor (below) uses a basic repeat pattern in a four by four arrangement, interrupted by a simple linear border. The regularity of the design is also alleviated by the delicate nuances of hue.

tively designed than other surfaces and objects – though there are notable exceptions to this generalization (*see* pp.71–2) – and Roman precedent has furnished tried and tested aesthetic solutions.

But whatever their inspiration, all floors must be hardwearing and most must be absolutely smooth, practical objectives that are best achieved through the indirect method (*see* pp.18–19), which will also encourage adherence to well worked out designs.

The bathroom floor (right) uses large-scale tesserae laid in such a way as to resemble the lines of setting of Roman floor mosaics. As is appropriate to the function of the room, a marine theme has been chosen that allows the mosaicist to create an underwater world beneath foot. Despite the organic motifs, however, this floor has been anchored by a strong rectilinear structure.

GRACEFUL GRECIAN FLOOR BORDER

This compact town-house conservatory is distinguished by an elegant mosaic floor border designed by Paris Ceramics in the classical 'Greek Key' pattern. With tesserae of matt blue-green and cream marble, it complements perfectly the French limestone flags used for the flooring, which are also left unvarnished so as to be in keeping with the texture of the mosaic. Such a simple and stylish border as this would be effective in almost any room of a house, but is particularly appropriate for halls and conservatories, where it invariably lends grandeur to a highly functional hard-stone floor.

To construct such an extensive repeat design by hand is possible, but is arduous and often thankless work. With functional mosaic of this sort it is generally preferable to buy the tesserae ready-made-up on strips of nylon or fibreglass. Don't worry unduly about this 'shortcut'; you will find that there is plenty of skill involved in adapting the pattern to fit the space available, and in the laying of the strips themselves. If you are not the sort of person who enjoys intricate and repetitive work, but love mosaic and the effects that it can create, then ready-made sections will be the answer to your prayers.

The mosaic floor border suffices as the single decorative element in this small conservatory (right). Its classical regularity creates a light, airy ambience that is opulent without being ostentatious.

Materials
Mosaic border strips
Anti-stain stone
  sealant
Cement
Sharp sand
Cement-based tile
  adhesive
Grout
Silver sand

Tools
Stanley knife
Hammer and chisel or
  hammer and hardie
Trowel
Wooden levelling stick
Lint-free cloth

1 Lay and seal the central area of the floor, ensuring that the edges adjacent to the mosaic border are clean and straight: here, brass strips have been stuck to the limestone with marble mastic. Have to hand the ready-made mosaic strips. If you are making your own, stick the individual tesserae face-up on to strong, flexible nylon mesh with resin glue and leave to dry thoroughly. Starting at the corners of the room, work strip-by-strip, measuring the space available then fashioning each length to fit by running a sharp knife over its backing material to remove those tesserae that are not needed. Lay the entire border without affixing it to judge the fit. Align the inner edge of the border; if the outer edge isn't exactly square with the wall, use a hammer and chisel or a hammer and hardie (*see* p.13) to cut infill tesserae. If you can't fit an exact number of repeats, 'cheat' the design slightly. This is best done by plucking out and replacing tesserae, sticking them down where needed with marble mastic.

2 Carefully set to one side the strips and seal their mosaic surface with matt anti-stain stone sealant. Mix the cement (*see* p.19), either straight or in combination with sharp sand (up to a maximum of 50%). Broadly spread on to the border area with a trowel. Then, using a wooden stick (the width of the border and the depth of the tesserae), level the surface. Leave to dry for twenty-four hours.

3 Apply a cement-based tile adhesive over the cement to a depth of 5mm (¼in), then use a clean trowel to press the strips firmly into this base. Complete the border, sticking down any infills with mastic as you go. Using a slightly damp cloth, wipe away any stray adhesive from the surface of the tesserae and leave to dry for twenty-four hours before grouting (*see* p.17). Here, silver sand has been added to the grout to modify its colour. Finally, polish with a damp lint-free cloth and seal the mosaic for a second time.

1

2

3

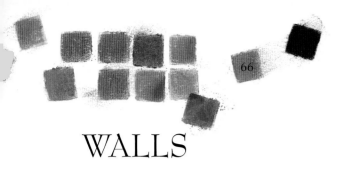

WALLS

Walls are perfect canvases for mosaic, which may be applied to them via the direct or indirect method (*see* pp.16–17 and 18–19). Using the former, the procedure is little different than for putting up ordinary household tiles, though the latter is preferable when large areas are to be covered with uniform tesserae. These may be bought ready-made-up on sheets and, if carefully customized by the replacement of some of the tesserae, allow strong, bold effects to be created.

Mosaic dados are particularly practicable in kitchens or bathrooms where splashes could damage paintwork, and the most pleasing effects can often be achieved with the simplest designs.

This testament of affection makes a striking and graphic statement, but is a simple design to execute. The black background mosaic tiles were bought ready-made-up on sheets, obviating the need for lengthy application one-by-one. A number of these tiles were then picked out and replaced by the white ones that carry the motif.

This Mediterranean-style bathroom uses opaque glass tiles to dado height that have been laid individually giving a slightly uneven surface. This effect is highly desirable, complementing the rough, mottled texture of the wall, and is enhanced by the thick, uncoloured grout that accommodates the irregularities.

A more daring approach is to decorate the wall not with any predetermined pattern, but with a random arrangement of tesserae applied directly. These may be shards of broken ceramic or even other materials, such as shells, stones, mirror or plastic objects, 'jigsawed' together to create a unique and unrepeatable surface.

A Middle Eastern flavour is exuded by this exotic bathroom due to the combined impression of the screen and the mosaic dado. A simple wave border is here made more complex by the hues and setting patterns of the background tesserae, and forms a strong but subtle decorative feature that blends well with the ornate marble tabletop.

A uniform blue mosaic ground is the perfect foil for controlled but opulent decoration. Classical restraint determines the plain rectilinear borders and makes all the more prominent the central motif: a rearing gold centaur.

Top: Cleo Mussi's one-off mosaic wall tiles offer instant charm and character to any kitchen or bathroom.

EXOTIC WALL PLAQUE

Materials
Tracing paper
Plain paper
Medium density
  fibreboard (MDF)
  or plyboard,
  approximately
  50 x 33cm
  (22 x 13in)
Wood sealant
Smashed crockery
Cement-based tile
  adhesive
Grout
Tempera or acrylic
  paint
Mirror plates

Tools
Pencils, paints and
  paintbrushes
Nippers
Flexible filling knife
Rubber gloves
Nailbrush
Dust mask

This wall plaque draws its inspiration from Islamic architecture and Indian textiles. In her distinctive, eclectic style, Cleo Mussi (*see* also pp.102–3), formerly a textile designer, creates a fantasy facade, based on a classical structure, but with an ogee arch surmounted by an enormous eastern sun. The material used is exclusively broken crockery but the style and technique make the piece appear encrusted with precious stones.

The serrated effect of the chipped glaze on the crockery tesserae of this plaque (above) gives the piece a satisfyingly rugged texture that is in keeping with its bold, original design.

1

2

3

1 Draw or paint your design to full size using as much detail as you need to establish all the patterns in the piece and bearing in mind the dominant colours of the smashed crockery available. Now trace off the main structural elements, keeping the tracing as simple as possible.

2 Trim a piece of medium density fibreboard or plyboard to the same size as the tracing. Seal the board and transfer the traced design on to it. Using the nippers to fashion the shapes you require, start to 'butter' the tesserae with cement-based tile adhesive using a flexible filling knife. Always infill after the main structural outlines have been completed and wherever possible use rim pieces at the outer edges. When the entire surface has been covered, including these edges, leave the piece to dry for 24 hours.

3 Wearing rubber gloves, grout in the usual manner (*see* p.17), adding tempera or acrylic paint as required (*see* pp.14–15). Then, wearing a dust mask, vigorously brush the grout off the surface with a nailbrush and leave to dry for a further 24 hours.

BATHROOMS

If properly grouted, mosaic can be just as practical as tiles in a bathroom or shower room, and can be used on walls, floors and surfaces with equal success. Indeed, it is in these rooms, with their delimited functions, that mosaic can truly run riot; justified by its practicality, it can cover enormous expanses that become, in effect, giant ceramic murals. At the other extreme, it can also be used for small-scale details; but even when this is the case, the customary sparseness of such rooms will ensure that any mosaic features are very prominent.

Individual mosaic objects are generally far more fitting for living rooms and bedrooms, and it is rare to find free-standing mosaic features in bathrooms. Mosaic elements tend to be 'designed-in' or else,

if they have been added, are fixed and permanent. This is perhaps why mosaic used in such rooms makes a strong design statement; the rooms seem wholeheartedly to have 'committed' themselves to the work.

Although bathrooms are highly functional rooms, they also tend to appeal to our creative instincts, providing the perfect environment for wild or whimsical decorations which we can admire as we float around in a relaxing froth of sandalwood bubbles. Themed mosaic schemes therefore come into their own and, for obvious reasons, marine subjects prove enduringly popular. There is the opportunity to indulge a private enthusiasm (as illustrated by the 'cosmic' bathroom opposite) or to recreate styles of the past – Roman- and Edwardian-style bathrooms are perennial favourites as these periods offer a wealth of distinctive design elements that can easily be plundered and adapted for the modern centre of ablutions.

A small-scale mosaic feature, such as this elegant basin (left), can be sufficient to elevate a fairly ordinary bathroom scheme. Here the colours and design of the object have been extended across the surface, but even were this not the case, the basin is so complete and pleasing that it could equally successfully stand alone. The design is simple, firmly structured and executed in a calm and limited range of harmonious colours. With a functional object of this sort it is essential to ensure that the tesserae adhere firmly to the base and that a water-resistant grout is used (see pp.14–15). For the sake of hygiene these tesserae should be as level as possible and the grout spread smoothly into every interstice. Clean with a non-scouring cream cleanser and disinfect regularly to be on guard against germs harbouring in any surface irregularities.

The exuberant shower room (right) is both playful and practical. Decorated with household tiles shattered into large shards, it uses the 'crazy-paved' technique to achieve an appealing staccato texture appropriate for the rhythmical and stylized 'cosmic' motifs. At first glance it appears a little Miroesque, an impression furthered by the serpentine curve of the mosaic edge that ascends the wall. Again, this effect is as functional as it is decorative, for it establishes a fully waterproof shower area that extends from floor to ceiling.

Because of the permanent nature of most bathroom fixtures and fittings it is important to think seriously about who should carry out the work. Although you might feel confident to cover a small, delimited area, you may find the idea of executing an entire room more than daunting. In these circumstances it is generally advisable to elicit help, be it from a professional mosaicist or a tiler. With the former you can expect a fair amount of design input (indeed this may be very hard to avoid), but with the latter probably very little or none at all. When working with either it is vital to keep in mind your own concept, and preferable to have recorded your design on paper. This may be modified during the process of consultation, but will nevertheless establish the parameters within which you expect the work to be executed. If possible, it is a good idea to view other sites that the contractor has already completed or at least ask to see a portfolio of work in the case of a professional mosaicist.

This Australian shower room has a fantastic 'floorscape' of abstracted marine elements including a hydra form, some white swimming sea creatures and, incongruously, an eye. It is divided by a blue-black 'reef' into two distinct colour fields that structure its arresting and unusual composition.

Here mosaic is used sparingly in a gentle scheme that owes something to the colour combinations of Pompeian works. The overall affect is extremely harmonious as different elements are carefully coordinated with each other: the wall colour is echoed by the mosaic border and the plain white tiling enlivened by shell and starfish 'tesserae'.

Just because the work is of an artistic nature, don't overlook the practical points, too. Consider the current state of the room, making a judgement about whether the plasterwork is sound enough to withstand the weight of ceramic cladding. Establish whether there is any damp, for this would in effect be trapped. Check that the room is well ventilated and that there is adequate and swift drainage, because excessive steam and humidity can encourage mould blooms to develop and any water standing in a pool on the mosaic may cause weakness and deterioration.

Think also of how non-mosaic elements are to be integrated into the scheme and, depending upon the mosaic materials that are to be used, for these need not necessarily be ceramic, evaluate the cements and grouts that will be most appropriate and durable – even carry out a small test to establish such important points as whether a smooth enough surface can be created (this is particularly important for shower room floors). Old white tile grout can become tatty, stained and grubby looking, so it may be wise to colour your grout or else apply the mosaic as tightly as possible.

If you intend to include organic elements in your scheme, such as shells, stones and starfish, scrub and disinfect these first to kill off any bacteria, dry them thoroughly and position them carefully so that they are neither a hazard nor likely to get damaged.

If you are likely ever to move from your property, think too about the likelihood of anyone wanting to inherit an unusual scheme and design it in such a way that it may relatively easily be removed without causing undue damage to the fabric of the room. A large

colourful panel fixed above your bath or placed above a vanity unit is one solution. Indeed, when creating a bathroom splashback (*see* pp.76–7), it is far easier to work on a backing board which can then be screwed to the wall when completed, and as easily removed, than to work directly on to the wall itself. Alternatively, a mosaic mirror frame will add individuality to a bathroom, and can easily be removed to decorate your new establishment when the time comes.

With its limited palette of blue, turquoise and green tesserae with occasional flashes of mirror glass, this French bathroom shelf looks almost like a choppy sea, an effect pointed up by the kitsch relief painting of a steam boat, which becomes the focal point of a jokey shrine to all things marine.

STUNNING STARFISH TILE

Tessa Hunkin of Mosaic Workshop (*see also* pp.28, 42–3 and 54–5) revels in the vibrant colours of vitreous glass. The strong linear starfish motif works splendidly with these hues, creating a bright marine image that would invigorate any bathroom tiling scheme. This project uses the indirect technique whereby the mosaicist places the tesserae face down and therefore works from the back of the object (*see* pp.18–19).

1

Materials
Craft paper
Ceramic floor tile,
30cm² (12in²)
PVA adhesive
Vitreous glass tesserae
Grout
Rapid-setting cement-
based tile adhesive

Tools
Charcoal
Scissors
Artist's paintbrush
Nippers
Rubber gloves
Jug
Squeegee
Sponge
Notched float
Lint-free cloth

1 Cut a piece of craft paper to the exact size of the ceramic floor tile. Using charcoal, which allows changes to be made, start to rough out the basic outlines of your design on to the paper. Mark the width of the border area by placing a complete tessera against each edge.

2 Choose the colours of the vitreous glass. Tessa has used four distinct hues, three of which are made up of two shades, a device that creates 'flicker' or 'colour texture'. Without gluing, lay one side of the border on the paper to establish the correct number and spacing of the tesserae. Mix the PVA adhesive with an equal amount of water

2

3

4

5

is uppermost. Leave this 'sandwich' for half an hour.

5 Using a wet sponge, thoroughly moisten the paper to loosen the PVA and gently peel the sheet back. Sponge the mosaic surface to remove any residual glue or stray grout and leave the piece to dry for a couple of hours (if you have used a rapid-setting adhesive; otherwise for as long as is recommended on the container). Regrout from the front of the mosaic, not forgetting to grout around the edge of the mosaic/ceramic sandwich. Fill any crevices, wipe with a damp sponge and leave to dry for thirty minutes. Finally, give the finished object a rub with a clean lint-free cloth.

and apply to the paper with an artist's paintbrush. Stick three sides of the border in place, remembering to stick the tesserae face down (were the fourth to be completed at this stage it would make it difficult to sweep out chips of glass). Then fill in the main starfish motif using quartered tesserae (*see* p.17). Glue down the outline

of the shape first, nibbling the tesserae to taper and fit the interior. Once the starfish is complete, fill in the frond motif using mainly halved pieces. Then lay the background tesserae keeping the majority whole but nibbling to fit around the 'flow lines' of the motifs (*see* pp.20–21). Lastly, complete the fourth side of the border.

3 Put the piece over a radiator or in a warm place to dry for approximately thirty minutes before grouting (*see* p.17), remembering that you are grouting from the back of the mosaic. Wipe the surface clean with a damp sponge, being careful not to saturate it, and put a board under the paper backing for support.

4 Wearing rubber gloves, spread an even amount of rapid-setting cement-based tile adhesive on to the smooth surface of the ceramic tile and key it using a notched float. Then lift the tile and lower it – adhesive-side down – over the mosaic. Firmly press upon the back of the tile to ensure adhesion. Turn the tile over so that the paper backing

FRESH FISH SPLASHBACK

Mosaic makes an attractive and effective water-resistant surface, so is ideal for use as a splashback behind taps in kitchens and bathrooms. A further example of Martin Cheek's vigorous work (*see also* pp.16–20 and 98–9), this piece has been executed using the direct method (*see* pp.16–17) and is composed primarily of vitreous glass. The tesserae are therefore highly manipulable and allow a relatively smooth surface to be created. The energy of the setting (*see* pp.20–21), however, more than compensates for any flatness in texture, as does the vibrancy of Martin's extensive and mixed palette of colours.

Materials
Medium density fibreboard (MDF) or plyboard (cut to fit the splashback area)
Vitreous glass tesserae
Smashed mirror glass
PVA adhesive
Water-resistant grout

Tools
Charcoal
Saw
Nippers
Mirror plates
Screws and screwdriver

1 Ensure that the medium density fibreboard or plyboard covers the splashback area exactly. Decide upon an appropriate motif (*see* pp.112–123), sketch out its basic outlines in charcoal and key the board with the teeth of a saw. Spread a selection of vitreous glass tesserae over the design and push them around until pleasing harmonies and contrasts are arrived at, remembering that colours need not be flat, but can be made up of a range of various tones. Smashed mirror may be useful for highlights in the background.

2 Using the nippers, divide a quantity of vitreous glass tesserae into halves (*see* p.17) and stick them around the depth of the board with PVA adhesive; divide a further quantity into quarters to create a three-tesserae deep border.

3 Slowly build up the motif, halving, quartering and nibbling the tesserae where necessary to describe the different forms. Now lay the background, nibbling those tesserae that 'hug' the motif, and setting radiating rows behind them to echo its shape (*see* pp.20–21). Complete the entire board and allow the glue to dry for one hour, then grout (*see* p.17) and leave for 24 hours. Finally, screw mirror plates to the back of the board (spacing with washers if the tesserae overhang) and attach the splashback to the wall.

1

2

3

KITCHENS

Cliché has it that the kitchen is the heart of a household, but sadly this is far from being the case in most modern homes. The pernicious flat-pack units have progressively inveigled their way into houses of all styles, making the kitchen 'laboratoryesque', practical but soulless, efficient but unwelcoming. The use of mosaic, even if employed to a very limited degree, cannot but personalize and invigorate the most sterile of interiors.

The essence of mosaic is non-industrial and individual; happily, it is difficult to use it in a standardized manner, and it is this very irrationality that makes it such a boon in kitchen schemes. All kitchens are, to some extent, predictable, in that the essentials are the same – sink, cooker, refrigerator and worksurfaces – and the introduction of distinguishing features helps to deflect attention from these somewhat dull, utilitarian objects.

This is not to imply that mosaic is impractical; it is, in fact, eminently suitable for kitchens, being strong, heat resistant and easily cleaned. Ceramic tesserae are the most appropriate, and, so long as the grouting is smooth and durable, share all the advantages of ordinary tiles. Moreover, mosaic is wonderfully opportunistic: able to spread across wood, metal and plaster with equal ease, and marvellous for covering design disasters of the past. Even unprepossessing 1960s and '70s fixtures can be made to look stylish and classy if a mosaic scheme is applied with thought. This face-lifting quality is of particular value when the owner wants to avoid the fitted kitchen option but is lumbered with some unattractive original features that may, however, be too useful to remove.

Despite the ease with which mosaic finds its place in the kitchen –

A day's work is sufficient to create a striking small-scale kitchen feature (left) that may or may not be accompanied by other mosaic objects in a similar style. The use of smashed plates is both an enjoyable visual pun and an effective design shortcut.

Through the use of mosaic this very ordinary kitchen (left) has been turned into a veritable pleasure dome – a temple to the senses in which colour, taste and texture are all enhanced and enjoyed. It is just this sort of kitchen that puts paid to the idea that you have to spend thousands of pounds in order to have a room you can be proud of, for this is the ultimate budget interior: the cabinets of the old plywood variety; the sink of unpretentious stainless steel; and the wall units straightforwardly home-made. Mosaic is also a budget option, particularly when broken china is used, which is perfectly in keeping with the ethos of this unusual scheme.

The designer has clearly been inspired by art-deco colours and shapes, so has intentionally left the fronts of the wall units open to reveal an astonishing array of polychrome ceramics. These are the key from which both the tiling and mosaic schemes below take their lead, the former using black and green tesserae, the latter black and yellow – controlled colour combinations reminiscent of the heyday of art deco design in the 1920s and '30s. This colour keying unifies a complex scheme.

ceramic is, after all, quintessentially a material of the kitchen – you would be well advised still to give a great deal of thought to the design of the scheme you intend to create, for a face-lift that goes wrong can be hellish to reverse. It is particularly advisable to keep your colour scheme under control, limiting your palette to specific hues, and to predetermine the areas that are to be covered rather than simply to let the mosaic spread like an uncontrollable rash over all the surfaces. If this is allowed to happen, the unfortunate result is that the room can appear messy and, more importantly, unhygienic. Regulated use of mosaic is therefore definitely the best policy for kitchen interiors.

KITSCHY KITCHEN SHELF

Candace Bahouth is a mosaicist with an extraordinary gift for creating combinations of colour and pattern that are unpredictable and which, though they seem likely to clash, in fact cohere into a 'Neo-'50s' style that is distinctively her own (*see also pp.40, 84 and 108–11*). Her quirky choice of crockery means that all sorts of motifs find their way into her work: here, tulips and a sunflower shape are paired to create a focal point at the centre of the shelf. And whatever the quality of the original crockery, it becomes interesting and attractive in its new context. The colourscheme is not rigid, though light and pastel shades are attractive choices for a kitchen setting.

Materials
Wooden shelf
Wood sealant
Ceramic tiles
Broken crockery
*Cement-based tile
   adhesive*
Grout
*Tempera or acrylic
   paint*

Tools
Drill
Hammer
Plastic spatula
2 Lint-free cloths
Nippers

1 Drill screw holes in the shelf and seal the wood. With a hammer, smash the ceramic tiles that will cover the ledge area and begin to lay them in a 'crazy-paved' fashion, using cement-based tile adhesive thickly applied straight from the tub with a plastic spatula. As you work, remove any excess adhesive with a damp, lint-free cloth.

2 Begin to apply the broken crockery over the back, sides and edges of the shelf, carefully mixing the colours and designs to create a lively overall pattern. Use the nippers to fashion exact shapes where necessary and try to apply smooth rim pieces at the edges. Don't put pieces over the screw holes; these will be concealed by grout at the last stage. Once the shelf is completely covered, leave it to dry for 24 hours. Grout in the usual manner (*see* p.17), adding tempera or acrylic paint as required (*see* pp.14–15). Polish with a damp, lint-free cloth and leave to dry for a further 24 hours.

1

2

EXTERIORS

Outward Appearances

❖

COBBLESTONE PATHS

GROTTOES AND
GARDEN WALLS

GARDEN
CONTAINERS

WATER FEATURES

Even the least promising small or shady garden can be invigorated and turned into a personal haven by the addition of appropriate mosaic features. Simple plant pots, containers and window boxes can be enough to create a unique and exciting atmosphere, and the combination of water and mosaic – for which there are very many possibilities – can have magical results, as is apparent from its use around ponds, on fountains and in luxurious swimming pools.

❖

A sunny conservatory or terrace offers the ideal opportunity for a mosaic feature built into a hard-stone floor. Here, a dynamic fishbowl design stands out in dramatic relief against a neutral grey background and seems to spread its vibrant colour up the column around which it pivots.

EXTERIORS: OUTWARD APPEARANCES

Mosaic is ideal outdoors for it is adaptable to just about any site. It may be used to embellish an individual feature or, in the form of pebble paths, run the whole length of a garden. It is durable, weather-resistant and may be applied in so many different ways as to make it the most adaptable medium for exterior decoration.

Whether beneath foot, on a wall or adorning a container or sculpture, an exterior mosaic should interact sensitively with its environment, seeking either to contrast with or complement the colours and textures of its surroundings. In a garden this may mean that its motifs consciously echo fluid and intertwined organic forms, whereas in a civic setting geometric abstraction may be more appropriate and striking. The tolerance of this interplay must be very finely judged if one is to avoid creating a blot on the landscape. Obviously, there are no strict aesthetic rules that must be adhered to, but a work that errs on the side of simplicity, humour or playfulness is generally a safer bet for a garden setting than one that attempts to make a grand statement.

Because the scale of exterior features differs so dramatically, there can be no generalizations about the type and extent of the work involved. The method for decorating a window box is very similar to that used for an ordinary pot (see pp.102–3), whereas the laying of a pebble slab or path involves a process developed specifically for exterior application (see pp.90–93). Consider carefully whether the technique you intend to use is appropriate to the function, siting and scale of the work, and make adjustments where necessary – for instance by increasing the size of the tesserae, using an indirect rather than direct method of application (see pp.16–19) or simplifying the design itself.

The manipulation of colour is particularly important in an outdoor setting but presents special problems because of the changing

A distinctive classical 'scalework' pattern is here created by row upon row of overlapping shells (below left). The technique is half tiling, half mosaic, tending towards the latter only because of the broken mirror-glass border which apes the effect of rain glistening on a rooftop. This detail and the pleasing patina of the wormcasts relieve the regularity.

Candace Bahouth's exquisite urn (below) is the perfect companion for her mosaic birdbath (see pp.108–11). Both have a wild exuberance, but are nevertheless very carefully attuned to the colours and forms of their garden habitat

– the mirror glass literally reflects the surrounding scene and ruby-red tesserae pay homage to the adjacent berries.

The extraordinary 'water shrine' (opposite) demonstrates just how individual the application of mosaic can be within a private garden. A bizarre combination of elements is united by a variety of mosaic materials, from mirror glass to whole ceramic tiles.

Steven Sykes' exotic fountain (left) uses brightly coloured and gold leaf tesserae in a number of interesting ways: as background, for which they are arranged in random colour juxtapositions; as border, for which the colours are graded by shade; and, at the back of the lower bowl, to create a sun-like design.

Cleo Mussi's wall plaque (below) makes a virtue of being sited on a very rough stone wall and uses a sun motif appropriate to its south-facing position.

But perhaps the greatest sun worshipper of all is Maggy Howarth, one of whose earliest works is this striking flaming-sun cobblestone path (right). The concentric patterns formed by the stones draw the eye to a central focal point (see also pp.90–93).

hues of the natural environment and the ever-shifting play of light. Harmonious or monochrome tones, such as those of cobblestone paths or terracotta tesserae, are unlikely to jar in any context, but do not offer as exciting a challenge to the pyrotechnics of nature as do vibrant smalti, gold leaf, mirror glass and highly coloured ceramic.

When using these brighter materials, key them to some relatively constant nearby element, ensure that they are situated so as to benefit from direct or dappled sunlight and take into account their visual impact from a range of perspectives. If these basic conditions are observed, it is unlikely that the mosaic will appear raw, crude or out of keeping.

COBBLESTONE PATHS

Pebbles are the earliest mosaic materials and there is evidence of their having been used decoratively from around the eighth century B.C. Later, from the beginning of the third century B.C., the Greeks constructed great pavimental mosaics composed of pebbles carefully selected for their colours, and even with the advent of multicoloured cubes (tesserae), the pebble survived as an important element in mosaic composition throughout the Hellenic period.

On a more quotidian level and in more recent centuries, cobblestone paths and pavements have become a feature of many towns and villages and are an excellent barometer of civic pride and local craftsmanship. Happily, this ancient art form and historic craft is currently

experiencing a renaissance with the commissioning of large-scale works for public spaces and the resurgence of interest in period design. Decorative cobblestone paths are appearing more frequently in town gardens, giving fresh appeal to large paved or concreted areas.

There are now, however, other highly contemporary issues to be borne in mind before such projects are undertaken, for it is vital that the pebbles come from sources that are not environmentally sensitive. It is no longer desirable to stage private raids when such large quantities of stones are required and permission should always be gained from the relevant landowner before removing any materials.

When gathering the stones, remember that colour and shape are the single most important elements and don't be distracted by textural subtleties that will not be perceptible when the path or pavement is viewed from a distance. Highly porous or soft stones will obviously

This elegant border design (left) employs a delicate classical pattern of scrolling foliage but uses the most dramatic contrast of pure black and white pebbles. The effect is formal and is particularly suitable for framing the beds of small flower gardens. Note that the pebbles in the border have been set directionally, but those that constitute the pure white infilled area have been laid at random.

A pebble parterre is an attractive option in a formal garden, and is, of course, very easy to manage. Here (left) brick has been incorporated into the design as the structuring element, almost in the same way that the Greeks used lead strips to differentiate separate areas of their mosaics.

The classical guilloche design (of two or more bands twisting over each other repeatedly) offers a neat border solution (below) for circular garden features such as posts, statues and large containers, the pattern resembling thick rope.

prove unsuitable so use only those that are hard and durable, such as flints and granites.

To lay a cobblestone mosaic of any size in situ is backbreaking and arduous work; it is therefore best carried out either by skilled workmen according to your design or, if by you, then constructed off-site in ready-made sections that can be assembled and laid relatively quickly (see pp.90–93). Because of the weight of the pebbles when they are set in concrete this process is never a one-man job, so be sure to have assistance to hand; and because of the scale of the work, it is wise first to practice on a small project, such as a threshold stone, path detail or an edging strip for a flowerbed.

COBBLESTONE PAVING SLAB

Maggy Howarth, originally a theatre designer, was first inspired to create pebble mosaics by the traditional patterned cobblestones that are still in evidence in some Lancashire villages, and the exceptional pavements she saw in Spain, Italy and Greece. Initially, she experimented with simple geometric designs, but soon moved on to large-scale works that included representational elements, such as stars, moons, suns, fish, birds and fantastic animals, all depicted in an extensive range of pebbles and stones. Part of her fascination with this type of mosaic

derives from her enjoyment of the stones themselves, which she collects in huge quantities (*see* also pp.86–7) and carefully sorts and grades according to their size, colour and shape. To a large extent it is these characteristics that determine the nature of the mosaics created, for the stones are the sole constituents of the artist's 'palette'.

In order to work in a studio rather than outdoors, Maggy has developed her own indirect method of cobblestone construction whereby sections are made in moulds. Although this procedure is neither technically complex nor demanding of unusual tools, it is an acquired skill, and a simple project such as a paving slab or threshold stone is the best idea for beginners. Cobblestone mosaics are likely to be significantly larger than the average work in glass or ceramic tesserae and, of course, far more unwieldy. Notwithstanding these practical restrictions, however, the results in this medium can be highly spectacular and can become real landmarks when permanently sited in paths and borders.

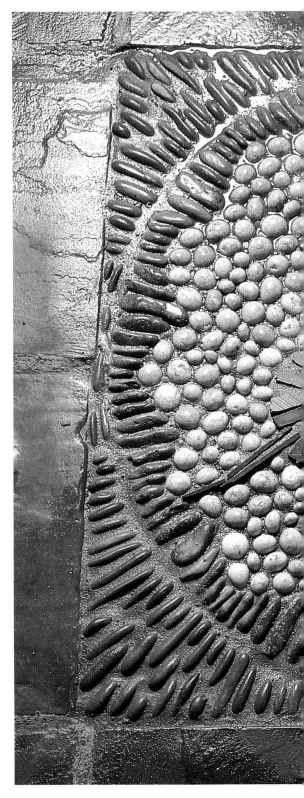

The finished cobblestone paving slab (left) is best bedded in a combination of dry sand and cement (in a proportion of three to one), then sprayed with a garden hose to add the requisite moisture to activate the mixture. It should ideally be set within a paved or bricked area as gravel or soil will tend to be kicked on to it. You may find it more convenient and attractive to set the slab within a square frame of pebbles, and these should be placed directly into the concrete as the slab is being laid.

The finished result, here seen after a sudden shower of rain, is an unusual and harmonious feature that will fit equally well into a town or country garden.

This polychrome body of a phoenix (far left), a detail from a larger cobblestone mosaic by Maggy Howarth, shows the huge range of colour and shape to be found in ordinary pebbles and demonstrates the importance of directional lines of setting.

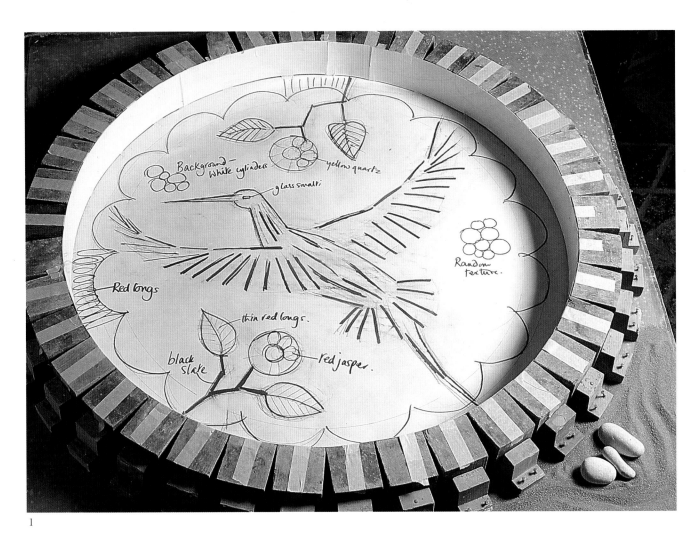

The annotated design within the mould, showing labels for: *Background – white cylinders*, *yellow quartz*, *glass smalti*, *Random texture*, *Red longs*, *thin red longs*, *black slate*, *red jasper*.

1

Materials

Hard pebbles
  (e.g. quartz, granite,
  limestone)
Pieces of slate
Dry sand
Non-stick cementitious
  grout
Cement
Aggregate

Tools

White paper, enough to
  cover a 90cm (3ft)
  diameter circle
Charcoal
Thick polythene
  sheeting
Wooden mould blocks
Hammer
Nails
Industrial pallet or
  thick board

Plastic card
Firm artist's
  paintbrush
Hand-held garden
  spray
Bucket
Shovel
Trowel
Wooden batten
Stiff household brush
Chisel

1 Wash and dry the
pebbles. On a large
sheet of paper, or
several pieces joined
together, draw a circle
approximately 90cm
(3ft) in diameter and
sketch the basic design
in charcoal. As you are
working indirectly, the
design will appear in
reverse on the finished
piece. Annotate the
design to identify the
different types of stone
and cover with thick
polythene sheeting.
Construct a circular
mould around the
design (over the
polythene) using blocks
of wood of at least
10cm (4in) high.
Hammer them securely
on to a small industrial
pallet or thick piece of
board. Secure plastic
card around the inside
of the mould. This will
prevent the cement
from sticking to the
wooden blocks.

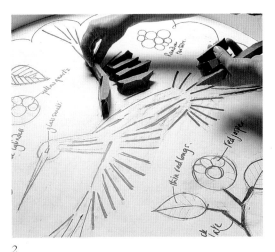

2

3

4

some of the stones will be almost completely submerged whilst others will protrude due to differences in length. Once the entire surface has been covered to a depth of 2cm (¾in), tap the base board to dislodge any trapped air bubbles and leave the grout for four to five hours to become putty-like.

5 Mix one part cement with three of aggregate and two of sand to a stiff, dryish consistency. (Allow for six large bucketfuls.) Shovel the cement over the grout, smoothing it down with a trowel until it is roughly level with the top of the mould.

Draw a long wooden batten over the surface, then tamp the cement down to encourage it to settle. Cover with polythene and leave for at least twenty-four hours (forty-eight if the weather's cold).

Remove the block supports and heave the slab over. Wash away the sand with water and a household brush. Now chisel off any stray bits of grout. Leave the slab to cure under polythene for four weeks before siting (*see* p.91).

2 Arrange the slates of the bird form over the design to practice manipulating their size and 'flow'. When you have completed planning the whole bird, remove the slates and sprinkle sand over the entire surface, obscuring the design.

3 Re-lay the bird motif, brushing away the sand with a paintbrush so that the slates lie directly against the polythene. Next lay the other motifs, then the border and finally the background. The pebbles should be upended (like inverted icebergs), imbedded in the sand but with only a very fine layer between their tips and the plastic sheeting. The sand between the slates and between the pebbles will determine how far out of the grout they protrude, so brush it up against the sides of the stones and keep it of an even thickness across the entire design.

4 Thoroughly and evenly wet the sand using a hand-held garden spray. Now mix about half a bucket of non-shrink cementitious grout (following the manufacturer's instructions but using sufficient cold water to make it fairly liquid). Pour it quickly and evenly over the stones, taking care not to displace the sand;

GROTTOES AND GARDEN WALLS

The essence of a grotto is that it should be fantastical and fun. Renaissance garden designers let their imaginations run riot to create extraordinary buildings elaborated with quaint rustic details. The seventeenth-century taste for garden conceits and eighteenth-century development of 'the picturesque' led to a sustained fashion for creating bizarre erections built to imitate caverns and caves. The craggy interiors of these structures, which sported such features as dripping water and stalactites, were often adorned with unusual rocks, shells, semi-precious stones and even pieces of mirror. The intention was that these should coruscate to create a magical environment, an effect that was often enhanced by the addition of dramatic, ambient lighting.

Few garden designers today would wish to contrive anything so artificial and extravagant as these theatrical creations of former centuries, but the desire to construct, invent and experiment remains undiminished, as does the impulse to embellish exterior walls and structures. So, though less sensational, grottoes and ornamented garden havens are still being built today in extremely personal and therefore widely varying styles.

Looking in through the window of this verdant grotto (above) reveals a highly decorative mosaic composition that is quite at odds with the rough exterior of the edifice. The work revels in its own incongruity, its creator clearly enjoying the fact that the sparkling and orderly space within is disguised from without. Executed exclusively in irregular (but carefully shaped) ceramic tiles, the

interior design is an inspired hybrid of classical, art nouveau and '20s style, displaying both great foliate arabesques and angular star shapes. The intended grandeur of the work is confirmed by the addition of the date, framed within a restrained mosaic cartouche.

Inevitably these tend to be both large-scale and permanent structures, so the investment in terms of time and money must be fully appreciated before they are undertaken. Unless mosaic is to be applied to an existing feature, it is likely that builders will be involved and this will generally prove to be the major cost. Designs are the key to progressing the work in a cogent fashion; without them you will be at the mercy of your contractors (and your own memory!). Remember too that any mosaic work will essentially be sculptural, being applied in three dimensions, so that the relation of planes and the effect from different viewing angles will have to be carefully considered and taken into account well before any project is undertaken.

If these hurdles are surmountable, enormous enjoyment can be had in the design and creation of a modern grotto that incorporates mosaic; for example, an alcove in a garden wall could be encrusted with shells and accommodate a built-in mosaic seat on which shell motifs are described by the tesserae; or a small rock pool could be surrounded by coloured and mirror glass and overarched by a mosaic canopy of vibrant smashed crockery.

The grotto has its roots in classical design for the Romans built themselves such features as garden vaults boasting extravagant water effects. In the seventeenth century the classical influence was very much a feature of European gardens, particularly apparent in the approaches to grottoes, which often consisted of elegant flights of steps leading to a colonnaded frontage.

Stephen Windsor Clive's mosaic columns (left) pay homage to Roman sources, both in their form and decoration, and he has used only authentic materials: pebbles, marble tesserae and uncut amethyst (above).

Cleo Mussi's sparkling wall plaques in smashed crockery and mirror glass lend an air of enchantment to a secret garden retreat (overleaf).

MEANDERING WALL SNAIL

Martin Cheek's interest in animation has led him to explore uses of mosaic that are humorous, playful and unexpected (*see* also pp.16–20 and 76–7). In this project, movement is represented by the silvery thread of mirror glass that mimics a snail's trail. The idea of a mosaic snail wending its slow way across a wall is in the grand tradition of garden ornaments and follies, the sole purpose of which is to decorate and amuse.

One might equally well choose to represent other insects or animals in this way, such as caterpillars, spiders and birds (*see* pp.112–123). It could also be interesting to create mosaic foliage – the ultimate evergreen.

Materials
Medium density
   fibreboard (MDF)
   or plyboard
Vitreous glass tesserae
Gold and silver 'ripple'
   smalti
Cement
Sharp sand
Smashed mirror glass

Tools
Brown parcel paper
Parcel tape
Nippers
Gum arabic
Trowel
Scalpel
Sponge
Lint-free cloth

1 Cut a piece of fibreboard or plyboard to a size significantly larger than you wish the snail to be (excluding its trail). Wet and stretch strong brown parcel paper over it, secured firmly with parcel tape. Now draw the contours of the snail on to the paper – in reverse as this project employs the indirect method (*see* pp.18–19) – and, using nippers, cut into quarters a few of the vitreous glass tesserae (*see* p.17), laying them in position to envisage their ultimate effect. Starting from the centre of the shell and spiralling outwards, use gum arabic to stick down the tesserae in a radiating pattern, remembering to lay each tessera face down (including the metallic ones). Nibble tesserae into tapered shapes to accommodate the curve of the shell. Complete the entire snail and leave to dry for at least one hour.

2 To prepare the wall, mix five parts of sharp sand with one part cement and add water until the mixture has a firm but malleable consistency. Then, with a trowel, apply

1

2

the mixed cement liberally to the area where the snail and its trail are to be situated, pressing it firmly into the bricks (or other surface). Remove any excess, flatten and key the cement with the point of the trowel and leave to dry overnight, covering it with polythene if there is a likelihood of rain or frost.

3 With a scalpel, cut the snail from the brown paper, leaving about 2.5cm (1in) clearance. Mix more cement and trowel a 1cm (⅜in)-thick layer over an area slightly larger than the snail (excluding its trail). Allow 10–20 minutes for the cement to get tacky, then push the mosaic surface firmly into it, patting the backing paper. Scrape

3

4

away any excess cement but don't remove the paper. Trowel a fresh 1cm (⅜in)-thick line of cement over the trail area and rapidly press the shards of broken mirror glass directly into it.

4 After three hours run a wet sponge over the backing paper of the mosaic and gently peel it off. Scratch away any stray cement from the surface of the tesserae and polish with a damp lint-free cloth.

GARDEN CONTAINERS

Whether you are decorating a window box, a small plant pot (*see* pp.102–3), a large urn, or a more unusual object, such as an old bath, sink or chimney pot, the attractions of outdoor containers are clear: the scale of each project is delimited; the final result is usually portable; and the combination of vigorous plant growth and mosaic is potentially very appealing.

   With all outdoor mosaic projects it is wise to use water- and frost-resistant cements and grouts (*see* pp.14–15) that will withstand the rigours of the weather, and to embed the tesserae as deeply as possible. With containers intended for planting, practical considerations such as these are of even more importance as their interiors will also be under stress from root growth and dampness. Ideally, when compost-filled, a container should be able to maintain enough moisture for the plant not to have to be watered daily, except in summer. Terracotta or clay containers are therefore best lined with smaller PVC or fibreglass pots that will improve water-retention and help to prevent excessive moisture that might encourage mosaic to fall off. If unglazed, these pots should be taken in or covered throughout the winter to avoid frost damage. Cement-based artificial stone, though more resilient, tends to lack the appealing patina of earthenware containers.

   All mosaic decoration should be sensitive to the scale of the container chosen and the ambient colours and shapes of its environment; it should avoid being too intricate and use tesserae that will enhance the base colour and texture of the vessel (*see also* pp.84–5) if it is to be only partially covered.

In the unusual garden (right) mosaic is the leitmotiv *that links the wall to other decorative elements, including this spherical earthenware pot. Some of the same colours and types of ceramic tiles have been used in both, but the abstract, geometric areas of colour are even more striking in the round where convexity exaggerates the play of light. Contrast is key here, both in hue and texture, as the sharp, flat shards of ungrouted yellow ceramic could not be more unlike the smooth skin of circular black tiles.*

The beauty of an idyllic mediterranean balcony is enhanced by the addition of an elegant earthenware vase (above) that sensitively echoes the texture of the whitewashed wall. Smashed crockery and terracotta combine effortlessly with the smooth organic forms of stones and shells to create a harmonious mosaic texture that flows down the vase in a series of gentle eddies.

STARRY PLANT POT

Cleo Mussi, one of the most inventive and highly respected of contemporary mosaicists, has worked on projects of all scales (*see* pp.24–5, 68–9, 85, 96–7 and 105), but particularly enjoys the challenge of the humble plant pot, for it is a *tabula rasa*, its mood and style defined only by the patterns, colours and textures of the mosaic decoration applied to it.

There is no reason why the pots you design should be any less distinctive than the one demonstrated here. Bear in mind that the pattern will have to compete with the foliage of the plant and don't be too discreet in your choice of motif; let the rhythms established by the tesserae used be strong and engaging. Basic geometric motifs are likely to be the most successful. You could try using a star, as here, but equally attractive results can be achieved with other clear, simple shapes (*see* pp.112–123). These may then be elaborated by the use of a variety of crockery, and even by the grout itself, which may be coloured to match or contrast with the rich pattern created (*see* pp.14–15).

For such small-scale projects really interesting tesserae can be employed, for one smashed plate is enough to furnish all the pieces you need of a certain colour or pattern. The use of domestic ceramics obviously becomes more problematic the larger the project, for rarely is one in a position to smash an entire dinner service. Smaller projects provide an excellent way of using up accidentally chipped or broken china, making it a 'green' process – and one therefore particularly well suited to plant pots and other small garden containers.

1

2

Materials	*Tools*
Terracotta pot	Small household
Household gloss paint	paintbrush
Broken crockery	Chalk
Water-resistant cement-	Nippers
based tile adhesive	Flexible filling knife
Grout	Rubber gloves
Tempera or acrylic	Toothbrush
paint	Lint-free cloth

3

1 Using household gloss paint, cover the pot evenly with your chosen colour, painting well over the rim and into the interior to give the impression of a full glaze.

2 With a piece of ordinary school chalk, loosely draw the basic outlines of the pattern directly on to the pot. (If your paint is of a light colour, use coloured chalk.)

3 Start to apply the broken crockery, smearing water-resistant cement-based tile adhesive thickly on to the undersides of the tesserae with a flexible filling knife. Use nippers to fashion the pieces to the exact shapes required (*see* p.17).

4 Leave the pot to dry for 24 hours, then mix a batch of grout (*see* p.17) coloured with tempera or acrylic paint (*see* pp.14–15) and, wearing rubber gloves, smear it thickly across the mosaic surface. Immediately brush away the excess with a toothbrush and, after 24 hours, polish with a lint-free cloth.

4

WATER FEATURES

For thousands of years water – from tiny trickles to enormous lakes – has invigorated gardens with its movement, sparkle, reflection and calming sound. Fountains, pools and water channels gained popularity in the thirteenth century and by the seventeenth century had become an essential and often playful element in many garden schemes: water jets were even directed to squirt up the skirts of women who inadvertently triggered them as they strolled past.

Today, with the advent of submersible electric pumps and flexible pool linings, the mechanics of water features are of less importance than their distinctive and attractive use, and mosaic has proved itself to be one of the most appropriate media for their decoration. Ceramic

and glass tesserae are generally weather- and water-resistant and can successfully cover both curved and flat surfaces. Additionally, mosaic used on such features affords the opportunity to respond to the natural colour scheme and the play of light on the water.

Small features are best for most modern gardens, and these may range from simple birdbaths (*see* pp.108–11), troughs and spouts to fountains, rills, mini cascades, ponds and pools. If shallow, the entire basin of the latter may be covered with mosaic, which becomes a liquid, mobile pattern when submerged; if deep, the edges may be lined with tesserae that reflect colour on to the water's surface.

Whether mosaic water features are prominent or partially concealed, thought must be given to the planting in or around them. Waterside plants offer unique qualities of texture and foliage, which should be exploited to the full: rushes, ferns, sedges and irises can be particularly attractive.

Mosaic water features have a distinct personality in a garden environment. From neo-Byzantine mysticism (far left) to Cleo Mussi's witty brutalism and 'stained-glass' polychromy (left and above), these examples show just how characterful individual treatments can be.

This walled mediterranean garden (left) encloses an oasis of sybaritic pleasure that is created by the use of an imaginative, erotic mosaic scheme. At the head of the pool two water nymphs, locked in an ecstatic embrace, are encircled by an art-deco style sunburst. This motif complements the bolder blue and black circular geometric design within the pool, which draws its inspiration from Roman sources. The folkloric figures of mermaids complete an eclectic ensemble, vaunting their pulchritudinous figures beneath the water. In this work a mosaic scheme transforms an ordinary rectangular pool into a highly distinctive private paradise.

The vast pool (opposite), though of an interesting shape, sits rather starkly within a paved and tiled terrace from which all greenery has been banished. Were it not for the visual excitement created by the enormous mosaic lining the floor of the pool, the overall effect might have been sterile and uninviting. As it is, the mystical, semi-abstract, semi-figural design chosen has a monumentality in keeping with the scale of the site, but also a delicacy of colour that makes the pool more approachable and inviting. The designer has responded to the reflections of the surrounding palm trees by creating a gentle play of foliage within the mosaic design itself, and this subtle echo helps to temper the man-made colours and textures of the terrace.

Few people can afford the luxury of a swimming pool decorated with mosaic, but the medium offers a stunning alternative to the standard treatment of blue or ultramarine tiles. Mosaic may be employed in a number of different ways: as an exotic border above the waterline or around the edge of the surrounding paving; on adjacent walls and steps; to describe motifs on the sides or on portions of the floor of the pool; or as a complete lining across its entire expanse. As the lining colour determines the apparent hue of the water, it is important to choose a design for which marine colours are appropriate, and one bold enough to withstand the distortions wrought by refraction and reflection.

RAZZLE-DAZZLE BIRDBATH

Candace Bahouth is a 'snapper-up of unconsidered trifles'; strange, quirky and kitschy ceramics appeal to her and she combines them in her unusual mosaics to stunning and often humorous effect. As a textile designer – a weaver by profession – she has an unerring eye for mixtures of pattern and colour and can create a unique, exciting mosaic surface from the most unlikely sources: remnants of a '50s coffeepot, a mass-produced tea-set and a nineteenth-century tureen may suddenly find themselves cheek-by-jowl (*see* also pp.40, 80–81 and 84).

A birdbath may seem an unlikely candidate for the attentions of so eclectic a mosaicist, but it is exactly this sort of solid, dependable, everyday object that attracts Candace. Its transformation presents an irresistible challenge: it is of a neutral colour so becomes a vibrant provençal blue; its form is simple and classical so is decorated on almost every available surface; it is intended for an idyllic country garden so is sprinkled with decadent ruby reds and flashing mirror glass. The resulting object embodies an extraordinary fusion of styles that, perhaps surprisingly, could not be more pleasing or attractive in cottage garden surroundings. Candace has produced an elegant and tempting blue swimming pool; the fact that it is for birds is both a gentle jibe at status-symbol culture and an act of homage to the rightful owners of the garden.

Candace works in a highly spontaneous fashion, predetermining the bare minimum of her design and delighting rather in the possibility of happy accidents and effects. When creating the tesserae her preference is to smash pieces of crockery with a hammer because this produces random shards of unpremeditated shape that may be quickly 'jigsawed' together. Their interlock need not be very accurate; indeed, this irregularity creates a very pleasing 'crazy-paved' effect that endows the piece with a vigorous, playful appearance. Gaps can always be infilled with smaller pieces and the whole mosaic united by grouting.

This startling blue birdbath (left) stands out in sharp relief against the greens and reds of an early spring garden yet is complementary rather than obtrusive. Its mosaic decoration softens its firm, classical contours and echoes the multiplicity of natural elements that surround it.

The edge of the basin (above) is bejewelled with rich red and green tesserae that are deeply embedded in a thick blue grout. The sumptuousness of this effect extends into the bowl itself, in which red tesserae are scattered like votive pennies across a sparkling swirl of mirror glass.

Materials
Mass-produced concrete birdbath
Crockery
Water-resistant cement tile adhesive
Tempera or acrylic paint
Smashed mirror
Exterior-quality heavy-duty paint

Tools
Goggles
Hammer
Rubber spatula
Nippers
Nailbrush
Lint-free cloth
Charcoal
Rubber gloves
Household paintbrush

1

2

1 It is important to work on an ordinary concrete birdbath that has not been treated in any way. These are available from most garden centres. Choose as simple a design as possible because the more convoluted it is, the harder it will be to apply the mosaic tesserae. Most birdbaths come in two or three pieces for easy transportation; each piece should be thoroughly dried out before work begins.

2 Wearing goggles, smash the crockery into largish shards using a hammer on a hard surface. Mix up enough water-resistant cement tile adhesive to cover approximately half the outer bowl (three parts adhesive to one part water). When you have a cake-mixture consistency, apply it directly to the bowl before fixing the tesserae.

3 Apply the pieces quite closely together in a jigsaw-puzzle arrangement leaving a border next to the rim. Small slivers can be used to fill any gaps, and nippers are helpful to fashion pieces when particular shapes are required. It is best to butter such infill pieces individually to ensure adhesion. Make any curves in the crockery follow the curve of the surface and don't leave any ridges sticking up as these can cut you. If you stop work, leave the bowl in a dry place. Mix more adhesive as required. Once you have covered the outer surface of the bowl, still leaving a border adjacent to the rim, let the piece dry for 24 hours at least and grout (see p.17) using the same adhesive mix coloured with tempera or acrylic paint. Use a dry nailbrush and then a damp lint-free cloth to remove the excess. Leave to dry until set.

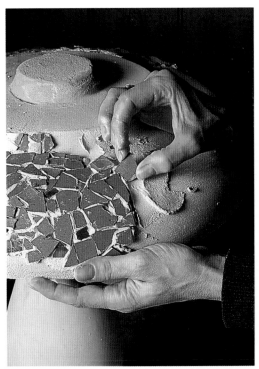

3

4

4 Sketch a spiral in charcoal on the inner bowl, then apply a line of smashed mirror shards over it, using a thick buttering of adhesive. Mirror breaks very sharply, even when nippers are used, so extreme care is required and goggles must be worn. Once the spiral is established, fill in the surrounding areas with smashed crockery, leaving the rim till last. Now sort out as many rim pieces as possible – i.e. those that themselves have rims – and apply these so that they slightly protrude above the inner and outer edges of the bowl. Then, using rectangular pieces without rims, fill the space between – the upper edge of the bowl – so covering the entire top area. Again, let the adhesive dry for 24 hours then grout the inner bowl and around and over the edge.

5

5 Having applied mosaic to any other areas of the birdbath that you wish to decorate (such as the base), paint the baluster column with an exterior-quality heavy-duty paint and allow to dry. Now leave the birdbath in a warm, dry place for at least three days. When thoroughly dry, polish the mosaic surfaces with a damp, lint-free cloth.

MOTIFS

Design ideas for mosaic can be derived from any number of sources, including photography, textiles and fine art, but it is often easiest to work from motifs simply depicted in graphic form. This section provides a handy range of just such design templates which, boldly drawn in black and white, offer a broad outline guide but don't predetermine the tesserae or colours to be used, the combinations of motifs or the objects to be decorated.

Regular, geometric designs are among the most simple to execute in mosaic. Their angularity is appropriate to what is generally a hard medium, and the fact that geometric designs tend to repeat allows the mosaicist to work relatively speedily. Often used for borders, they may encircle or enclose representational motifs to great effect.

Stylized floral motifs may involve slightly more complex cutting than geometric designs (*see* previous page), but nippers can generally be used to taper and curve the edges of the tesserae. Remember too that the impression of a curve can be created optically out of a series of straight edges set at an angle to each other. Don't be afraid to use grout to plug any gaps that occur, but mix in a colourant where necessary to avoid these becoming too prominent.

Mosaic was one of the principal media used by the Greeks and Romans (*see* pp.8–9) for the embellishment of walls, floors and even entire pavements. There is therefore an enormous wealth of classical motifs that remain extremely popular with mosaicists today.

Animal motifs are among the most frequently used in this medium (*see* pp.54–5, 90–3 and 98–9) and are extremely effective if kept simple. As the Mexican border (below) demonstrates, their familiar shapes are still recognizable even when highly schematized.

Stars, suns, moons and planets are very powerful motifs imbued with a potent symbolic content. They are equally appropriate for small objects to which they lend a spiritual dimension and for large schemes that benefit from their strong graphic appeal. Cupid (opposite), though neither astronomical or astrological, has a similarly mystical presence; according to mythology, his influence extended over the heavens, the sea and the earth.

Marine subjects tend to be used for bathroom interiors (*see* pp.63 and 71–7) but are very versatile and easily adapted to a range of applications.

Even a small number
of different marine
motifs ranged around
a bathroom can create
a very evocative,
themed interior
cheerily redolent of
sun, sea and sand.
They are also
particularly effective
on boxes and other
small objects
(*see* pp.46–9).

GLOSSARY OF TERMS

Acrylic paint A water-based paint that may be used to colour grout.

Base The support for mosaic tesserae. Your choice of base material will vary depending on various factors, such as the location and size of the work and the tesserae used (*see* p.14). Popular bases include medium density fibreboard (MDF) or plyboard, wood and cement.

Bolster blade The alternative name for a hardie (*see* Hammer and hardie)

Buttering The application of adhesive to the back of a tessera.

Cement Used both as a base and as a medium for bonding tesserae to a base. Its durability makes it ideal for outdoor projects (*see* p.14).

Cement-based tile adhesive An adhesive used for sticking ceramics and glass to wood, synthetic and other materials.

Cement dye Used to colour cement.

Ceramic tesserae Usually the cheapest tesserae available, ceramic tesserae can be fashioned from a wide range of unglazed or glazed ceramic materials, including household tiles and broken crockery.

Direct method The most basic and common technique for the laying of mosaic. Tesserae are cut and stuck, face up, directly on to the base. The surface of mosaics made using this method are not always smooth, and much license can be taken with the shape and texture of tesserae (*see* pp.16–17).

Emblemata Intricate Roman representational panels inserted as focal points into floor schemes.

Epoxy resin An extremely strong adhesive used for sticking glass and ceramic to metal. The resin must be mixed with a hardener before use to chemically activate the bonding agent.

Gum arabic A temporary water-based adhesive that can be used to bond tesserae to paper, gum arabic is often used when making mosaics by the indirect method (*see* pp.18-19). Wallpaper paste is generally a suitable substitute.

Grout A cement mortar.

Grouting The process of applying grout over the surface of a mosaic to fill in the interstices between the tesserae, thus creating a smooth, more durable surface.

Hammer and hardie Tools used in conjunction for the cutting of mosaic tesserae. A tessera ready to be cut is placed on the hardie, a small metal block with an anvil-shaped edge that is usually tungsten-tipped and embedded in a block of wood. The hammer, which is large and sickle-shaped, is then brought down squarely on the tessera, cleaving it in two.

'Hockey-stick' framing wood A framing moulding.

Hydrochloric acid An acid used in mosaic work for dissolving away excess cement or grout.

Indirect method A mosaic laying technique often used for large-scale work intended for outdoor sitings. Tesserae are stuck face down on to paper with a temporary, water-based bonding agent, generally gum arabic or wallpaper paste. The mosaic can then be transported if necessary, whole or in sections, and set in its permanent base with the paper side uppermost. The paper is then peeled away to reveal the finished work. The resulting surface is usually smooth, and best grouted.

Infill tesserae Chips of tesserae used to fill in small gaps.

Interstices Gaps or spaces between tesserae.

Jigsaw Type of electric saw suitable for relatively intricate cutting.

Keying To key a base is to roughen a smooth base surface with a sharp implement, often a saw, in order to create a surface that is more receptive to tesserae.

Latex additive A rubberizing agent added to cement-based adhesives to give flexibility and movement.

Marble mastic An adhesive used for sticking marble to most surfaces.

Mosaic cutters An alternative name for nippers (*see* Nippers).

Mosaic strips It is possible to buy ready made up strips of mosaic on which the tesserae are attached to nylon or fibreglass backings. They are relatively simple to lay and are ideal for large-scale works, or those in which repetitive patterns are required (*see* pp.64–5).

Nibbling Using nippers to cut away tiny fragments of a tessera to achieve a precise shape.

Nippers A tool for cutting glass and ceramic tesserae. Usually tungsten tipped for extra strength, nippers are ideal for fashioning tesserae into exact shapes.

Notched float Also known as a 'serrated float'. A rectangular trowel with a smooth surface and a serrated edge used in mosaic work for levelling and keying cement.

Opus tessellatum A Roman mosaic technique whereby regular, square tesserae are applied in a rectilinear arrangement. The resulting uniform design was most frequently used to fill expanses of background.

Opus vermiculatum A Roman mosaic technique whereby tesserae are arranged in rows around the main mosaic motif to create a halo effect and emphasise the setting lines of the design.

PVA Polyvinyl acetate, an adhesive used for sticking glass or ceramic to wood, fibreboard or plyboard.

Pattern paper Dressmakers' paper used in the indirect method (*see* pp.18-19). Layout paper or brown parcel paper may be substituted.

'Ripple' smalti Glass tesserae having a thin but irregular layer of gold or silver sandwiched between thick and thin layers of plain glass.

Serrated float *see* Notched float.

Silicone sealant An adhesive used for sticking ceramic to glass and most other surfaces.

Silver sand Can be added to grout to modify its colour.

Smalti Traditional mosaic tesserae manufactured in Italy that may be bought in large 'pancakes' and cut with a hammer and hardie, or else bought precut as somewhat irregular rectangular chunks of opaque glass.

Tempera A water-based paint that may be used to colour grout.

Tesserae The basic building blocks of mosaic. The term embraces diverse materials, including stones and pebbles, glass, broken crockery, fragments of ceramic and mirror glass.

Vitreous glass Manufactured opaque glass tesserae, square with a bevelled underside to aid adhesion. The range of colours available is more limited than for smalti, but vitreous glass is reasonably cheap and very durable.

Water-resistant cement-based tile adhesive Adhesive used for sticking ceramics and glass to metal or concrete that is more suitable for external use.

ACKNOWLEDGMENTS

PROJECT CONTRIBUTORS

Candace Bahouth
Bathroom mirror, p.40; Kitschy Kitchen Shelf, pp.80–1; Garden urn, p.84; Razzle-dazzle Birdbath, pp.108–11
Ebenezer Chapel, Pilton,
Somerset BA4 4BR. Tel: 07498 90433

Emma Biggs
Tartan Tabletop, p.28; Mexican Terracotta Mirror, pp.42–3
The Mosaic Workshop, Unit B,
443–9 Holloway Road, London N7 6LJ
Tel: 071 263 2997

Zoë Candlin
Gaming Table, p.29; Jazzy Abstract Tabletop, pp.32–7
After Noah, 121 Upper Street,
London N1 1QP. Tel: 071 359 4281

Martin Cheek
Chessboard, pp.16-17; Paving slab, pp.18–19; Punch Flip, p.20; Fresh Fish Splashback, pp.76–7; Wall Snail, pp.98–9
53 Pursers Cross Road, London SW6
Tel: 071 731 0241

Ray Halsall
Jewellery, pp.50–1; Glitzy Glamour Earrings, pp.52–3
14b Cressida Road, London N19
Tel: 071 272 5164

Maggy Howarth
Flaming sun cobblestone, p.87; Cobblestone Paving Slab, pp.90–3
Cobblestone Designs, Hilltop,
Wennington, Lancaster LA2 8NY
Tel: 05242 74264
(Maggy Howarth is the author of *The Art of Pebble Mosaic*, Search Press, 1994)

Tessa Hunkin
Diaphanous Butterfly Brooch, pp.54–5; Stunning Starfish Tile, pp.74–5
The Mosaic Workshop, Unit B, 443–9
Holloway Road, London N7 6LJ
Tel: 071 263 2997

Cleo Mussi
Red Tailed Monkey with Green Sideboards, p.24; Dresser, p.25; Mosaic wall tiles, p.67; Sun motif wall plaque, p.85; Exotic Wall

Plaque, pp.68–9; Grotto wall plaques pp.96–7; Starry Plant Pot, pp.102–3; Garden fountains, p.105
Unit 72, Top Floor, Abbey Business Centre, 15–17 Ingate Place, London SW8
Tel: 071 498 2727

Paris Ceramics
Roman floor design, p.62; Graceful Grecian Floor Boarder, pp.64–5
583 King's Road, London SW6
Tel: 071 371 7778
(Grecian floor border pp.64–5 laid by Gilby Construction, The Surrey Canal Office, Rope Street, London SE16 1TE
Tel: 071 394 9444)

Stephen Windsor Clive
Intricate Octopus Casket, pp.46–9; Mosaic columns, pp.94–5
Real Mosaic, 51 Aldensley Road,
London W6 0DJ. Tel: 081 741 3218

PICTURE CREDITS

2 Marie Claire Idées (Hussenot/Chastres/Lancrenon); 3 Jean-Francois Jaussaud; 7 Clive Nichols (designer: Daniel Pearson, pots Cleo Mussi); 8 left Archiv fur Kunst und Geschichte, Berlin; 8 centre Agence Top (Rosine Mazin); 9 Archiv fur Kunst und Geschichte, Berlin; 10 left Ancient Art & Architecture Collection; 10 right J.P. Godeaut; 11 Archipress (Luc Boegly); 21 left Ancient Art & Architecture Collection; 21 below right C.M. Dixon; 21 above right E.T. Archive; 22–23 Lanny Provo (designer: Deborah Yates); 24–25 Marie Claire Idées (Hussenot/Chastres/Lancrenon); 24 Cleo Mussi; 26 Rebecca Newnham; 27 designer Heather Burrell (photography by John Glover); 28 left Christian Sarramon; 30 Lanny Provo (designer: Deborah Yates/Raymond Jungles); 38–39 Rebecca Newnham; 40 centre Marie Claire Idees (Chabaneix/Chabaneix); 44 Rebecca Newnham; 45 The Peter Bailey Company (photography by Jan Baldwin);

51 Jacqui Hurst (designer: Julie Arkell); 56–57 Stylograph (Morin/Côté Sud); 58 C. David Livingston (designer: Bauer Louann); 59 Esto (photography by Scott Frances); 60 left Henry Bourne; 60 right Christian Sarramon; 62 right Paris Ceramics; 63 Vogue Living (Bathroom designed by Alice Whish); 66 right Tim Goffe (designer: Peter Cocks); 66 left Trevor Richards; 67 left Paris Ceramics; 67 above right IPC Magazines Ltd/Robert Harding Syndication (Rapid Eye); 67 below right Vogue Living (Bathroom from the home of Nicholas Feuillatte); 70 J.P. Godeaut (designer: Martin Lionel Dupont); 71 Belle Magazine (photography by Simon Kanny); 72 Australian House & Garden Design Series Magazines (photography by Russell Brooks); 72 right Belle Magazine (photography by Peter Rad); 73 Marie Claire Maison (Chabaneix/Chabaneix/Bastit); 78–79 Gross and Daley; 78 Marie Claire Idées (Hussenot/Chasstres/Lancrenon);

80–81 The Garden Picture Library (photography by J.S. Sira, designer Daniel Pearson); 82 83 Lanny Provo (designer: Barbara Hulenicki/Carlos Alvarez); 84 left James Merrell; 85 Nadia Mackenzie; 86 left Nadia Mackenzie; 86 right Cleo Mussi; 86–87 World of Interiors (photography by Philip Sayer); 88–89 Vincent Motte; 88 Stylograph (Millet/Côté Sud); 89 Stylograph (Touillon/Côté Sud); 94 Deidi von Schaewen; 100 Marie Claire Idées (Maltaverne/Faver); 101 Lanny Provo (desinger: Deborah Yates/Raymond Jungles); 104 Nadia Mackenzie; 104–105 Cleo Mussi; 105 The Garden Picture Library (photography by J.S. Sira, designer Daniel Pearson); 106 J.P.Godeaut (designer: Martin Lionel Dupont); 107 Lisl Dennis (From Morocco by Lisl & Landt Dennis. Photographs copyright © 1992 by Lisl Dennis. Reprinted by permission of Clarkson N. Potter.)